Desktop Publishing
A Management Report

A J Marlow

NCC Blackwell
MANCHESTER • OXFORD

British Library Cataloguing in Publication Data

Marlow, A. J. (Andrew J.)
Desktop publishing: a management report
1. Desktop publishing. Applications of microcomputer systems
I. Title
070.5'028'541

ISBN 0-85012-688-6

Published for NCC Publications by NCC Blackwell Limited.

Editorial Office: The National Computing Centre Limited, Oxford Road, Manchester M1 7ED, England.

NCC Blackwell Limited, 108 Cowley Road, Oxford OX4 1JF, England.

Typeset in 12 point Times and printed by Hobbs the Printers of Southampton.

ISBN 0-85012-688-6

Preface

This report has been compiled for managers of organisations who require a background to the subject of desktop publishing, and may need guidance in piecing together a strategy for selection and implementation of the technology.

As with any computer industry related topic, keeping pace with new developments is difficult. The massive competition between suppliers of software and hardware forces the rapid introduction of new facilities, the enhancement of existing products and the design of systems offering increased performance. Those individuals who took advantage of the early desktop publishing technology have seen the market expand rapidly and successfully in a very short space of time. This causes two problems for the novice. Firstly, by now so much has happened in the field of desktop publishing, since its emergence on the microcomputer market, that a great deal of catching up has to be done. Secondly, there is no slowing down of the trend as yet, so by the time you think you have caught up, another solution to your publishing requirements has been developed.

Apart from the problems for the novice, the production of any literature on the subject is likely to become outdated in a short space of time. However, there must be a starting point for the newcomer to the technology, and for the manager who may not require specific details about individual features of products in order to instigate a plan for acquisition of the technology. This publication aims to provide that start point.

Throughout the text, I have attempted to tackle the scenario of desktop publishing acquisition, based on practical experiences. Wherever possible, I have tried to bear in mind the fact that technology moves ahead, and to concentrate on the broader knowledge required to make effective decisions about the acquisition of a desktop publishing system. However, this does not mean that one can exclude specific examples of current products. Indeed, certain products have been given coverage in this publication to give examples of a particular application, level of technology or machine type. The products mentioned are by no means intended to be recommendations for any particular application.

In addition to mentioning particular products, you will also find some prices and costs of desktop publishing components. Like the products themselves, prices are subject to constant change. In most cases, as time goes on, these prices come down. It is important for you to understand that the prices and cost examples in this publication are meant as illustrations of particular scenarios, based on prices that were appropriate at the time of publication. The prices quoted are not the recommended retail prices, and may vary considerably from one supplier to another. If one is to illustrate the effect of pricing on decision making, and on the selection process, then an example must be provided as a basis for the point being made.

In Appendix B, the information provided was correct at time of publication, but may be subject to change without notice from the publisher. You are advised in all circumstances where seeking additional information about products and services, to make enquiries of your local computer retailer, or to seek professional assistance from a consultant. The trade press will also provide a source of information, and the weekly and monthly publications will keep you up to-date with current trends in the industry.

This publication should provide you with sufficient background information on the subject of desktop publishing to enable you to seek further help in a much more informed way. In the computer industry in particular, you are at a disadvantage if you have not done some 'homework' before attempting any major acquisition of hardware and software. There are plenty of retailers who will try to capitalise on that disadvantage.

Finally, I have attempted to present this text without favour to any type of manager or organisation. The content applies as much to a non-commercial establishment, such as an educational authority, as to a commercial enterprise. However, the desktop publishing market itself recognises that the largest share of the sales of the technology is in the private sector and, consequently, the examples and features of desktop publishing tend to be geared towards a business environment.

A J Marlow MSc
Titchmarsh, 1989

Contents

1 Introduction

During 1984, as Publications Manager of a large software company, I investigated the new technology associated with publishing to see what benefit it may be to the organisation in which I was employed. I had to visit companies and independent consultants to discuss the technology – what it was and what it could do, and the costs, both of purchase and operation, and to examine the forerunners of what was to develop into a very big market within only two or three years. As a result of this investigation, which led to several demonstrations of the technology, numerous meetings, reports to the board of directors, feasibility studies and cost justifications, a decision was made to implement various publishing solutions to meet the needs of the company, and these measures were introduced in stages.

This publication represents what, as a manager, I would like to have been able to do had I known then what I now know of the subject five years later. As with any new technology, there is a great deal of sorting and shuffling of products, standards and development which makes the process of decision making about the acquisition of such technology a trifle 'hit and miss'.

Desktop publishing is still a fast growing development and, as such, is forever offering new ways of solving old problems. If you are a manager in an organisation with the responsibility for acquiring and/or implementing desktop publishing in some form, then you will need a basic understanding of the subject, sufficient for you to make valued judgements. In this respect you have a considerable amount of information available, unlike the situation even a few years ago. The problem today is that there is so much information, that it is difficult to see the wood for the trees. The choice in the market is now considerable and, consequently, so is the competition. So, in addition to a report which gives you background information about the subject, you need something which clarifies the various options from an independent viewpoint.

A DEFINITION

Generally, desktop publishing can be described as the use of an electronic system, usually based on microcomputer technology, for the purpose of producing high-quality printed matter which may include text, lines and graphic images.

This is achieved by the use of either standard business computer hardware (such as computers that may be employed for business accounting or word processing) or a special 'dedicated' computer system, desktop publishing software and a printer capable of high-quality output of both text and graphics.

Dedicated computer systems are simply those that are designed to be most suitable for a particular task, for example because the keyboard includes special function keys. The need for a printer that can produce graphic images as well as letters and numbers excludes the use of daisywheel printers, which have been traditionally used for high-quality computer printouts, from being suitable output devices for desktop publishing. In their place a relatively new type of printer has emerged – the laser printer – which produces a page of printed matter in a similar way to a photocopier, using plain paper and toner. The hardware is discussed in more depth in following chapters.

The possible combinations of the aforementioned components are quite considerable. Which type of system you choose will depend upon what you are trying to achieve, and this means more than just what sort of output you want. You may be trying to achieve a number of goals, which may include the following:

- to improve the quality of printed matter
- to decrease the timescale of producing documents
- to reduce the cost of publishing and printing
- to increase profitability
- to remove the dependence on external resources
- to investigate the potential of new methods
- to offer staff the potential for developing new skills
- to improve morale
- to match the image of your competitors

- to replace old technology
- to replace staff
- to increase sales
- to keep within a budget
- to learn about publishing fundamentals

Some of the above may seem obvious, others closely related and some may be reasons for using desktop publishing that you would not have considered relevant. The fact is that all of the above, plus other factors, are indeed relevant to the implementation of desktop publishing, and, as a manager, you should be looking at all possibilities. Even if you are specifically aiming at one of the above, you should take time to consider other factors as well, since these may influence your choice of system, or whether in fact you even decide that desktop publishing is a viable proposition at all.

Desktop publishing has been described as not simply 'fashion software' but one of the great breakthroughs in personal computing, as innovative and important in its field as the first spreadsheet or word processor, both of which are now in widespread use throughout all sectors of business and industry, education and government authorities. It is difficult to balance the argument about whether it is better to wait for such a new market to settle down, and perhaps to then take advantage of much more comprehensive systems at lower prices, or to gain as much experience as possible as soon as possible. It is intended that this document will help you to make your choice.

Acknowledgements

The author wishes to thank all those who have helped in the production of this book, including Brenda Durndell and those at NCC.

2 History and Basic Principles

To publish something is to make it 'public'. By printing, any number of copies of a document or picture can be produced quickly from one original. In order to publish something, there are various fundamental stages one goes through:

- Copy Preparation
- Editing
- Setting
- Printing

Each of the above stages, together representing the basics, has many sub-stages in its own right. Copy preparation involves authoring of the content of the document. The word 'copy' is often used to refer to text and/or pictures which form the original content of a publication, rather than meaning a 'duplicate'. So, if printers ask you for the 'copy' of a document for publication, they mean the words or pictures of the original.

Copy preparation might involve one of a number of techniques. It may begin with a hand-written text, typed, dictated notes, etc, with perhaps illustrations in the form of line drawings, photographs and so on. Once originated, there is usually some degree of editing required to ensure that the content is grammatically correct and conveys its message well.

Having prepared the copy, some initial design considerations may be made, even on the simplest publication, from a letter to a magazine. Design may be nothing more than considering the position of the text on the page, how long a page might be, or whether to use an underlined heading.

Except for very basic reproduction in the form of photocopying, the copy usually needs some additional work to make it presentable. When a publication is to be printed, this usually involves the 'setting' of the text. Text setting or, more accurately, typesetting involves producing a version of the copy which is more presentable, visually attractive and readable.

Once the copy is 'set' it is generally referred to as artwork, and from artwork all other stages form part of the print process.

To help the reader to understand all of these stages, the following few paragraphs provide a potted history of publishing and printing techniques. The achievements of modern desktop publishing are simply a degree of automation of the basic principles, though much of the original terminology remains.

A POTTED HISTORY

As early as the 7th or 8th century AD, the Chinese carved wood blocks, with a reverse image, raised in relief, of the text or illustrations to be produced. These blocks were inked and paper was then pressed on to them. 'Moveable' blocks, or type, each carved with one individual character were introduced later in the 11th century. These allowed a combination of characters to be put together, and then taken apart and rearranged for the next job.

Moveable Type

Printing with moveable type, cast from metal – a universal and basically unchanged method of printing until the 1970s – was pioneered in Germany in the mid-15th century by Johann Gutenberg. Until the 19th century, metal type was cast by hand, and individual pieces of type were 'set' manually to compose words. Both of these tasks were slow. By 1838, a mechanised process of type-casting was introduced by David Bruce in New York. By 1884, a machine called the linotype, patented by Ottmar Mergenthaler in the USA, enabled an operator, selecting letters from a keyboard similar to that of a typewriter, to compose whole lines of text at a time.

Lithography

If a publication was to include an illustration, these were still hand carved from wood or etched into metal. Pictures that did not have to be printed with letterpress text (text set from raised letters) could be reproduced using a different method called lithography – a technique invented by Aloois Senefelder in Germany in about 1798. Lithography depends upon the fact that grease repels water, and the printing surface used is flat (unlike letterpress). The image was originally drawn in reverse on a flat stone with a greasy crayon, then the stone was wetted. Repelled by the grease, the water dampened only those parts of the stone not covered by the image. Then greasy ink was applied with a roller. The dampened surface repelled the ink, which stuck only to the parts covered by the unwetted crayon. Therefore paper laid on the flat stone picked up the image from the crayon surface. When the paper was peeled off, the stone could be re-inked and more copies made. The technique survives today, except that thin metal plates have replaced the flat stone.

Photolithography was introduced in France in approximately 1852, when a photograph instead of a hand-drawn image was used to provide an original picture. In the process, light passes through a negative or positive onto a metal plate with a light-sensitive coating. After chemical treatment of the plate, a hardened deposit is left in the form of the negative or positive image. When typeset text was photographed and included on the illustration plate, simultaneous photolithographic printing of text and graphics became possible, and by 1960 had become a serious rival to letterpress. Today, photolithographic printing is now so widespread that it is difficult to find many other forms, except perhaps in high-quantity newspaper and magazine printing which uses another method called photogravure. This is a highly specialised and expensive process.

Half-tones

By the 19th century, a new technique, the half-tone process, enabled photographs to be reproduced in magazines and newspapers for the first time. Shades of grey from a black and white photograph were conveyed with parallel black lines varying in thickness according to the shades of the original photograph. In the 1880s, the American Stephen Horgan introduced a dot-screen system for half-tones still used today. This gives a sharper picture than lines because the picture can be broken down into smaller pieces. All illustrations, not simply photographs, could be reproduced in the same way.

High-speed Printing

By making printing plates more flexible they could be fixed to cylinders, allowing continuous printing on rolls of paper by using what was called the rotary press. Much faster than pressing one flat sheet at a time, this process became adopted for all high-speed printing and was especially suited to newspaper production. Although the high-speed printing process has been around since the mid-1800s, the process of setting the text was geared to type-casting, and typesetting methods had changed little since Gutenberg's day.

Computers in Typesetting

By the 1970s, the introduction of computerised typesetting was to change everything. The reporter on a newspaper, for example, was able to compose a story on a keyboard, recording the text on magnetic media, and seeing the story appear simultaneously on a video screen. From this, the computer could be used by an editor to typeset the text. Instead of producing the text as physically cast lines of characters, the typesetter produced an image of the text using a photographic technique, printing out the typeset copy on a special paper. The computer could control the different styles and sizes of characters electronically and this opened up a completely new opportunity for design and accurate reproduction.

Whole pages could be assembled by taking the separate outputs from the typesetter and pasting them into place with any half-tone illustrations accompanying them. The whole page 'artwork' could then be photographed for the photolithographic printing process.

Computerised Page Make-up

In still more advanced technology, the computer was to provide the means for making up the whole page layout on the computer's screen, thereby removing the need to physically paste up the components of a page (like headings, columns, etc). Half-tones and other illustrations still had to be added afterwards to finish the artwork.

The continued and rapid development of computer technology was to provide the final automation in the page make-up process by allowing photographs and other illustrations to be broken down into dots using an electronic scanning process. Once stored in this form they could be electronically manipulated and included in the page on the computer screen, and printed out simultaneously with the text to form complete artwork ready for the print process. Artwork at this stage is referred to as 'camera ready', meaning that it is ready to be photographed to make the printing plates.

Desktop Publishing Arrives

Today, desktop publishing has brought the page make-up process onto the personal computer; a machine that can conveniently occupy space on a normal office desktop – hence the name of this new technology. By replacing the complex computers used for page make-up in the late-70s with specially written software on modern business microcomputers, the entire process of typesetting, picture and graphics manipulation and camera ready artwork production was made available to everyone.

With the introduction of a new sort of printer – the laser printer – which could produce high-quality artwork on plain paper using the same technique as a photocopier to print an image using toner (fine black particles that adhere to the paper under pressure and heat), not only could the operator of a desktop publishing system produce the artwork required for printing but, for relatively small print runs of limited colour, print the copies themselves. This truly brought publishing and printing up to-date.

Early DTP

When I first saw a desktop publishing application, it was on a computer called the Apple Lisa. The Lisa had an attribute that made it different to all other microcomputers I had seen and used. The design of the screen layout was such that the background was white, and the text and other images on the screen were black. In other words, it resembled type on a piece of paper. Unlike most other word processing systems, the text displayed not only the words, but the typeface (the style of the text), the size of characters and all other attributes which represented what the finished document would look like if it were printed on paper. A second characteristic of the Lisa was that the operator demonstrating the use of the computer and software was using a small hand-held device, connected to the computer by a lead, which was moved around on the desktop surface. The movement of this device was being echoed on the screen as a small pointer or arrow moved in synchronisation with the moving of the device. The device was called a mouse. This was because its size and shape were sort of mouse-like.

The Apple Lisa itself was connected to a phototypesetter and it provided the operator with a means to effectively control the output of the phototypsetter, by being able to see the image accurately portrayed on the computer screen. The ability to preview the output of the phototypesetter was not in itself an innovation, but what made the Lisa so special was the way in which the screen responded immediately to the operator, displaying text and graphics the instant they were added or amended.

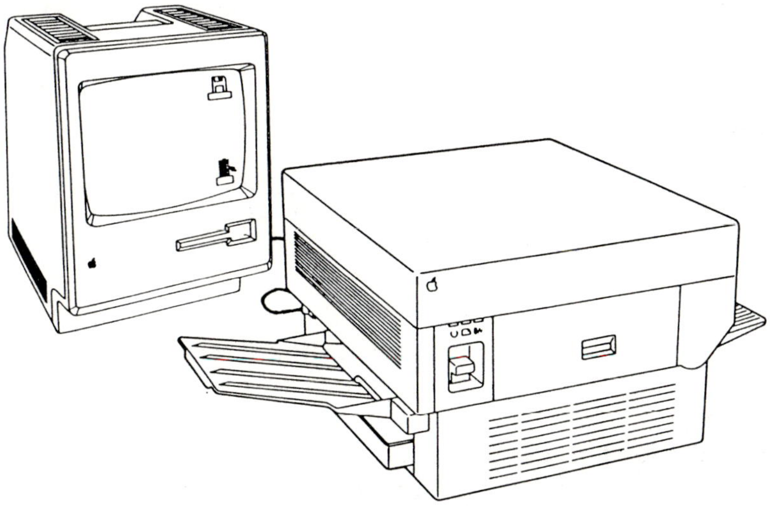

Figure 2.1 Apple Macintosh and Laser Printer

The Apple Lisa never really made an impact in the microcomputer market, but it gave rise to what was to be the forerunner of all desktop publishing systems and remains one of the most popular choices of system – the Apple Macintosh (see Figure 2.1). The technology that surrounded the computer, which made use of the mouse device as well as a keyboard for communicating with the machine, and the special way in which the screen used black text on a white background, made the Apple Macintosh an ideal vehicle for the development of software to control publishing-related functions.

Since then a rapid proliferation of alternative systems has all but saturated the market. However, the basic principles involved have not changed dramatically since the first Apple Lisa, and most computers using desktop publishing software emulate the style and operation of that innovative machine.

BASIC PRINCIPLES OF DTP

For many newcomers to the subject, the purpose of desktop publishing is not always easy to distinguish from that of word processing. One tends to think of the creation, manipulation and output of text (otherwise called 'copy') from a computer system to a printer as word processing.

With desktop publishing, in order to improve the appearance of the output, instead of using a dot matrix or daisywheel printer, one sends the output to a typesetter. A typesetter may be a laser printer or a phototypesetter, both of which can be viewed as providing an enhanced quality output. This enhanced output lends the text a more 'authoritative' appearance, often making it more readable (ie easier on the eye). How the system achieves this enhanced output may be, to the operator, somewhat irrelevant. What is more important are the facilities that enable the operator to control the content and layout of a document by setting tabs, margins, page lengths and so on. Why, then, is desktop publishing something different to word processing?

Comparing DTP to Word Processing

The process of preparing text for publication using a computer, requires the facilities for the keying in, editing, manipulation and arrangement of the words themselves. The copy preparation stage of any publication, whether it is a letter, report or brochure, is concerned mainly with the content, and not with the appearance or layout. A word processor can provide the means to do this, and by using the editing capabilities of a word processing software system, a draft document can be 'polished' ready for turning into artwork. Spelling checkers are a useful additional facility provided by word processors; and, for lengthy documents, the ability to be able to handle large amounts of text – which can be typed in quickly and efficiently – means that a computerised word processor makes an ideal tool for the job.

A desktop publishing system, though it does literally 'process' words, is largely concerned with the appearance of the text, its positioning on the page, the size and style of the characters, the inclusion of pictures and other illustrations – in fact with all the elements of what are collectively described as page make-up. A desktop publishing system is basically a page make-up utility. Since most page make-up systems display their layout on the screen in much the same way as the document will ultimately appear when printed on paper, the computer needs to do a lot of processing to display text in different styles and sizes – and with the display of graphics, such as photographic images, even more.

Standard word processors do not concern themselves with the appearance of the text as such, even though they may be capable of printing the output in various styles. Instead, the screen display tends to be much simpler again, concentrating on the content rather than appearance. The consequence of this difference between the two is that desktop publishing systems do not make very efficient systems for original text entry. They are slow to respond to the keying in of new text because they take time to present the styles and sizes of the page layout on the screen while the text is entered. For original text preparation then, standard word processors are preferred. Most desktop publishing systems rely upon the copy having already been prepared on a word processor. The text already stored in magnetic form on a disk can then be 'read' by the desktop publishing software, and styles can be attached to the text to define the page layout.

The same process applies to the manipulation of graphics. Desktop publishing systems, while they are able to cope with presenting and printing graphics such as line drawings, scanned photographs and the like, are not in themselves very suitable for the origination of the graphic images in the first place. Like text, the desktop publishing system relies upon a separate facility for the production of the graphic images – a graphics software system, for example, or a special piece of equipment used to convert a photograph into a computer image using electronic means.

So a desktop publishing system is distinguished from a word processor on the basis that it acts as a tool to place the elements of a page layout (text, graphics, logos, etc) within a predefined print area, and to define the styles and sizes of the elements in order to maximise the quality of presentation and to most effectively convey the messsage contained within the text.

There is a slight confusion, however, over the fact that the result obtained from using a desktop publishing system, if specifically designed for page make-up, can in some cases be equally well produced using a sophisticated word processor. Such word processors are those that have taken the facilities of the basic system of text entry, editing and manipulation, and added extended features to control the style and presentation of the pages beyond that of their more traditional counterparts. The subject of different types of desktop publishing systems is discussed in more detail in Chapter 3, Classification of DTP.

Page Make-up and DTP

The illustration in Figure 2.2 emphasises the basic page make-up principle of desktop publishing – the manipulation of various design elements and text to make up a whole page layout. Before technology permitted this work to be done using a computer, these separate elements had to be manually positioned on a page. Typeset text cut into appropriate lengths, pictures and other graphic elements, such as rules and boxes, all had to be pasted onto a layout board (a piece of cardboard, often with a fine graph-like grid for accurate positioning which did not reproduce when the artwork was photographed for platemaking).

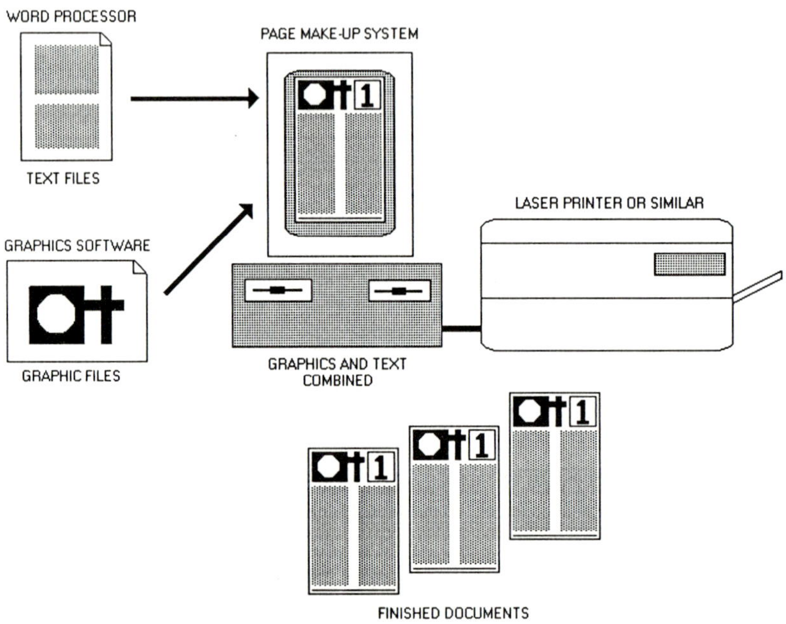

Figure 2.2 Principle of Page Make-up

For those print and design establishments that do not yet use the page make-up facilities of a computer-based system, this method is still adopted. It is also common to find a combination of these techniques, where the printed output of a desktop publishing system provides the basic layout and organisation of all the text elements; and where graphics such as photographs and logos are pasted on afterwards.

Style Control

Desktop publishing systems all provide control over the style of text and page layout. Some provide finer control than others. Depending

Aster Medium
Aster Italic
Aster Bold
Aster Bold (Slanted)

Avant Garde Gothic Light
Avant Garde Gothic Light (Slanted)
Avant Garde Gothic Medium
Avant Garde Gothic Med. (Slanted)
Avant Garde Gothic Bold
Avant Garde Gothic Bold (Slanted)

Baskerville Roman
Baskerville Italic
Baskerville Bold
Baskerville Bold Italic

Bembo Medium
Bembo Italic
Bembo Bold
Bembo Bold Italic

Bodoni Medium
Bodoni Italic
Bodoni Bold
Bodoni Bold Italic
Bodoni Black
Bodoni Black (Slanted)
Bodoni Black Condensed
Bodoni Black Condensed (Slanted)

Case Fraction (Serif)
Case Fraction (San-Serif)

Century Old Style Medium
Century Old Style Italic
Century Old Style Bold
Century Old Style Bold (Slanted)

Century Schoolbook Medium
Century Schoolbook Italic
Century Schoolbook Bold

Clarendon Medium
Clarendon Medium (Slanted)
Clarendon Black
Clarendon Black (Slanted)

Ehrhardt Medium
Ehrhardt Italic
Ehrhardt Semi-Bold
Ehrhardt Semi-Bold (Slanted)

Garamond Medium
Garamond Italic
Garamond Bold
Garamond Bold Italic
Garamond Ultra
Garamond Ultra (Slanted)

Gill Sans Light
Gill Sans Light (Slanted)
Gill Sans Medium
Gill Sans Medium (Slanted)
Gill Sans Bold
Gill Sans Bold (Slanted)
Gill Sans Extra Bold
Gill Sans Extra Bold (Slanted)

Helvetica Light
Helvetica Light (Slanted)
Helvetica Medium
Helvetica Medium (Slanted)
Helvetica Bold
Helvetica Bold (Slanted)
Helvetica Black
Helvetica Black (Slanted)
Helvetica Light Condensed
Helvetica Light Condensed (Slanted)
Helvetica Medium Condensed
Helvetica Medium Condensed (Slanted)
Helvetica Bold Condensed
Helvetica Bold Condensed (Slanted)
Helvetica Black Condensed
Helvetica Black Condensed (Slanted)

Figure 2.3 Sample Typefaces

on what you are trying to achieve, the facilities may or may not be adequate for the job. The decision-making process to determine which desktop publishing page make-up system to use requires careful consideration of your intentions.

All DTP systems will provide common basic functions. These include the ability to select a style and size of typeface. The typeface is the design of the characters which affects the appearance of the text. Typefaces are designed to be attractive but they do require careful selection so that the choice does not impair the readability of the document. The typeface then, is the style of the characters used for the text. Typefaces have their own names and design characteristics, and a complete set of characters in a particular typeface – for example all letters, numbers and special characters – is called a font.

The illustration in Figure 2.3 shows a selection of typefaces, their sizes and names. Desktop publishing systems offer the operator a choice of typefaces and sizes to use in a document layout, though the variety offered will depend upon many factors, including the type of printer and any other output device being used, the capabilities of the software, etc.

One document may contain more than one typeface; for example, headings will often be of a larger type size and sometimes in a different style to those of the body text of the document. Using different typefaces adds character and interest to the appearance of the document. Even something as basic as a mailshot letter can be made more acceptable and interesting by the appropriate selection of typefaces and sizes. Care has to be exercised, however, so as not to over-use such facilities. But with appropriate training and experience, an operator can improve upon the appearance of documents that were previously confined to the typewriter or standard word processor.

Apart from the style of the type used in a document, a page make-up system will provide facilities to set up tabs, margins and columns, into which the text can be fitted to make the organisation of the various text elements interesting and informative. Newsletter-style documents will probably tend to copy the style of a newspaper, with text placed in two or more columns on a single page, unlike typical book style which has only one single column. Multiple-column manipulation of text is a unique feature of desktop publishing page make-up systems, one which could not be adequately provided for by word processors.

There is a fundamental difference in the use of spacing with typesetting from any typewriter. With typesetting, all the characters have an amount of horizontal space which is proportional to the actual width of the character, so over a large amount of text, it is quite noticeable how much less space is needed to fit text into a predefined space. Typewriters and word processors that, on the other hand, use daisywheel printers tend to use non-proportional spacing. So the letter 'i', for example, will occupy the same amount of horizontal space as the letter 'm', even though the 'm' is a wider character.

All desktop publishing systems offer proportional spacing of text and this is one of the fundamental differences between typeset text and non-typeset text.

This paragraph of text has been set using a non-proportional typeface. Every character has the same amount of horizontal space. This makes it easy to line up columns of figures, for example, when producing a table, but the typeface does not make optimum use of the space on the page.

Graphics

In addition to the control over the appearance of the text, desktop publishing systems generally provide a number of features that enable graphic elements to be included in the text. These include rules (vertical and horizontal lines) boxes, shading, etc. These elements can be used to improve the appearance of the page further; for example, a rule might be used between the columns of text in a report to separate them. Some desktop publishing systems provide a number of functions for limited drawing capabilities, but more complex pictures generally need to be produced using a different system, and then 'imported' into the page make-up system to be positioned on the page as required.

Output Devices

The output devices supported by various desktop publishing systems can vary. Most now offer output to a laser printer – a high-quality printing device that allows typesetting of text at a fraction of the cost of phototypesetting, though the phototypesetter remains the ultimate quality. This book has been typeset on a laser printer. Dot matrix printers also feature as output devices, and all three types are capable of handling different typefaces and graphics. Further discussion on the various output devices is provided in Chapter 4, Technology Developments.

Methods Employed

There are several ways in which a page-make process can take place. In some cases, a certain amount of the style control of a document can be predefined in the original word processed text before it reaches the desktop publishing software. In other cases, a desktop publishing system will take raw text and every attribute to do with the style of the text and the page layout has to be manually controlled. How various desktop publishing systems actually carry out the process of page make-up depends upon the 'type' of system. The various classifications of desktop publishing systems are examined in Chapter 3.

3 Classification of DTP

INTRODUCTION

Desktop publishing can be broken down into a number of categories. These relate to the degree of capability of the system and therefore ultimately the purpose for which they are intended. As a general guideline, the different categories are separated into four groups:

Group I - Word Processor-based Systems

Word processors that can produce a varied layout, can control the size and style of the typeface, and with sufficient intelligence to produce output on a laser printer or high-resolution output on a dot matrix printer.

Group II - PC-based Page Make-up Systems

Simple and advanced page make-up software systems, designed to run on standard personal computers, which enable text and graphic elements from external systems (such as word processors and drawing software or scanners) to be combined in a page layout, and to provide control over the appearance of output which may be on a dot matrix printer, laser printer or phototypesetter.

Group III - PC-based Electronic Publishing

Also page make-up software systems designed to run on standard personal computers, but offering a much higher level of function than those in Group II, generally by providing better typographical control of the design and thc manipulation of page elements.

In most cases, systems in this group are capable of output to a variety of typesetting devices, including digital phototypesetters and laser-controlled page printers.

Group IV - Dedicated Electronic Publishing Systems

Systems offering a similar level of function to those in Group III, but on hardware which is dedicated to the purpose of desktop publishing. These systems tend to have an advantage for professional users, by providing specialised keyboard layouts to facilitate manipulation and selection of specific typographical functions, the use of paper-sized screens (A4 and A3) and tailored software features.

The systems in each of these groups provide some overlapping features. It is not always easy to differentiate between adjacent categories of desktop publishing, though the differences between, for example, word processing-based DTP and dedicated electronic publishing systems are usually considerable.

WORD PROCESSOR-BASED DTP

Word processors capable of producing a certain degree of layout control over standard typewriter-style document production, are now offering features very similar to those of basic desktop publishing systems. Consequently, in this group of software systems, it is difficult to differentiate DTP from word processing. Such word processors are able to take advantage of the capabilities of output devices such as laser printers, to produce character styles of different typefaces and simple graphics. Some offer the ability to produce documents of multiple-column format, allow picture images to be included and other similar page make-up functions, but they retain the facilities that make word processors most suitable for original text entry and manipulation – such as spelling checking, search and replace of words or phrases, cut and paste (moving blocks of texts within the document) and other similar editing features.

In order to control the style of the printed output, such systems may use a coding system in which commands that control the style, size and position of text and other elements are 'embedded' within the text file, and these commands are interpreted by the output device when the document is printed

Such systems are not necessarily cheaper than desktop publishing software, but since most page make-up systems rely on the use of a word processor anyway, the overall cost may be less. For staff used to the operation of word processors, such systems are easier to operate in the short term, since they use familiar methods of text manipulation. The setting of tabs and margins, page lengths, headers and footers, for example, is not unlike that with any standard word processor.

If the application for which the system is to be used is limited to the production of high-quality letters and reports, then the word processor based systems can be most adequate.

With such systems, the appearance of the text on the screen often does not represent the output style. Figure 3.1 shows an example of a word processor screen. All characters are the same size and style, though the output associated with the document may be quite different. Software systems that do show a reasonably accurate representation of the page layout and styles on the screen (as if the screen were the printed page) are known as WYSIWYG systems, which stands for What You See Is What You Get. Figure 3.2 shows a screen layout which is WYSIWYG. While some word processor-based systems offer this WYSIWYG facility it is commonplace within page make-up systems.

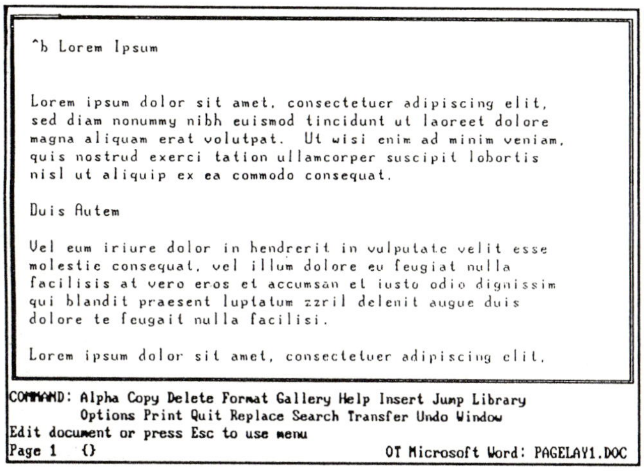

Figure 3.1 Standard Word Processor Screen

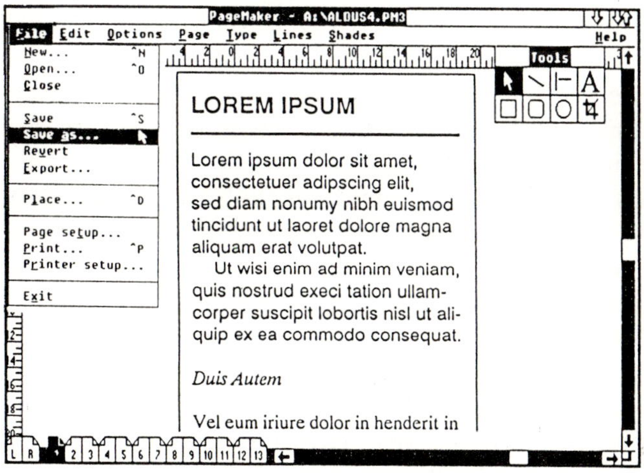

Figure 3.2 WYSIWYG Screen

PC-BASED PAGE MAKE-UP

As previously explained, the basic principles of desktop publishing revolve around the process of page make-up. In this context, the basic elements that comprise a document, the text and any associated graphics, are produced externally to the page make-up software. Text will have been generated on a word processor, and stored as a file on the computer disk. The file is then read by the page make-up software and the text placed into a page layout accordingly. Different word processors store their text in different formats, ie any information (indents, page breaks, etc) stored with the words themselves may be encoded in the file, and the system of encoding used by one word processor will not necessarily be the same as that of another.

Consequently, page make-up systems need to be able to read or recognise a variety of text file formats. Those of the most commonly sold word processors are generally catered for. Since many word processors can output a 'straight text' file known as an ASCII file (one which has no special format codes at all), and page make-up systems can always read this, there is usually little difficulty in transferring word-processed text to the desktop publishing system.

In a similar way, pictures produced by graphics software packages store images as files on the disk. Like text files, different graphics systems store picture images in different formats. Again, a page make-up system must be able to recognise and read the various formats in order to be able to include an image within the page layout.

Once the elements of the page layout are within the control of the desktop publishing software, they may be manipulated to produce the final page layout. For text, this means specifying typefaces, styles, sizes and spacing for headings, paragraphs and the like. For graphics this may mean sizing and positioning.

The underlying structure of the page layout may be defined separately without the need of the text and pictures that will be included with the final printed document. This process is called *defining a style sheet*. A style sheet comprises all the attributes that describe how the page elements will be arranged and displayed: for example, the size of columns into which text will be placed, the size of the page itself, the typeface to be used for headings, sub-headings, paragraphs, etc. Once a style sheet is defined, the text and pictures can be called into the page make-up system and after final adjustments and manipulation, the complete document can be printed out.

Page make-up systems store the complete document as a 'publication'. How this is actually done varies from one product to another. For example, the original text (word processed) and graphics files may be left intact, and the completed document stored as a separate file. Alternatively, the publication may be stored in a number of separate files – text in one, graphics in another, style sheet information in a third, and so on.

Because style sheets hold information relating to the design and layout of the document, but do not necessarily include any 'content', they may be used for the production of many documents that require a similar style. Under these circumstances, style sheets are often referred to as 'templates'.

Some of the most popular page make-up systems provide a facility to enable a word-processed document to be prepared for page make-up, to an extent which reduces the amount of work that would otherwise need to be done on the document to assign the various style attributes.

For example, the following attributes may be assigned to a main section heading of a report:

Text:	centred
Typeface:	Helvetica
Style:	bold
Size:	18 point
Spacing beneath:	2 lines
Special:	begins a new page

These, and other, attributes can be assigned to a simple code or name; for example, H1 for a level 1 heading.

Now, within the same document, a sub-heading may have slightly different attributes:

Indent from left:	10mm
Typeface:	Times
Style:	bold
Size:	12 point
Spacing beneath:	1 line

As with the main heading, this heading may be associated with the code H2 – a 2nd level heading.

The body of the document – the paragraph text (often referred to in page make-up systems as 'body text') – will have yet another set of style attributes:

Indent from left:	10mm
Typeface:	Times
Style:	Roman
Size:	10 point
Spacing beneath:	0

This may have a name such as 'body text'.

Having assigned the styles to the style sheet and given them names or codes, the text within the word-processed document can be prepared to include the style information. For example:

> [H1]Section 1 - Sales Report
>
> [H2]1st Quarter Performance
>
> [body text]Compared to the results of previous years, the sales in the same quarter this year have been encouraging. With three additional representatives in the field, we have been able to offer more personal support services to existing customers as well as extend our market penetration in those areas targeted in the sales budget report...

The codes and names used, such as H1, H2, body text, etc, are generally referred to as 'tags'. They are enclosed in non-standard brackets or are preceded by a little used character, such as @, so that the desktop publishing system can differentiate them from the normal text. The names used will match the names of the styles defined in the page make-up software, so when the code [H1] is encountered, for example, it knows that the following text is to adopt the styles set up under that name. The style will then only change when another style code is encountered.

Figure 3.3 shows the example above after processing and output from the page make-up system. There are various terms associated with this technique – generic coding, text style code embedding, document tagging, for example. The principle is particularly helpful for the copy preparation of long documents which have a fairly simple style. If the document is complex in layout and design, using such preparation techniques is not really practical.

> **Section 1 - Sales Report**
>
> **1st Quarter Performance**
>
> Compared to the results of previous years, the sales in the same quarter this year have been encouraging. With three additional representatives in the field, we have been able to offer more personal support services to existing customers as well as extend our market penetration in those areas targeted in the sales budget report...

Figure 3.3 Example After Processing

Another distinctive feature of page make-up systems is the manner in which the operator 'communicates' with the software package. The use of the WYSIWYG screen style is one aspect of this. Another is the use of a special device called the mouse: this device, when moved about on a desk surface, sends co-ordinate instructions to the computer which affect the position of a 'cursor' or small arrow on the screen. This cursor can determine the point of insertion for new text, or move an element on the screen from one place to another. It may also be used in combination with the keyboard to select options from the screen, and select text for the purpose of assigning attributes of style, for example. Most page make-up software utilises, what are called, 'pull-down menus'. These are lists of options that can be displayed on the screen using the pointing device to select (see Figure 3.4).

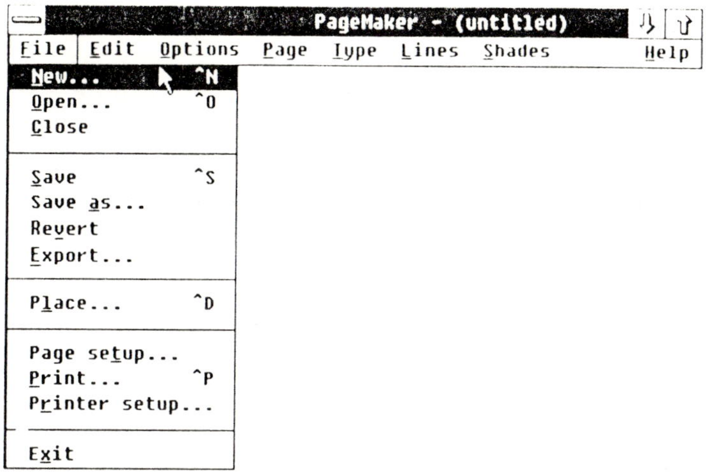

Figure 3.4 Pull-down Menu

Indeed, the association of the mouse pointing device and desktop publishing systems has made them almost inseparable. Some PC-based page make-up systems cannot function without the use of a mouse, others may be usable without them, but cumbersome. By contrast, they are not generally used in the word processor based systems, and the systems of group III and IV, which tend towards professional typesetting, do not make much use of the device either, as explained in the following paragraphs.

ELECTRONIC PUBLISHING

Electronic publishing is a term often used as a substitute for desktop publishing. It does, after all, describe the same process of publishing with a computer. But the term is also used to express the difference between 'professional' publishing and general use. The general application of desktop publishing tends to cover the use of PC-based page make-up software, used on generally available personal computers which may also be used for other applications, and where publishing is not the primary concern of the organisation or department using the system. Desktop publishing is, in this respect, an embellishment to word processing, and occasionally employed to produce good-looking reports, overhead transparencies, price lists, letters and other sundry business-like documents.

Similar systems would also be used by educational establishments for teaching the basics of the technology and for general-purpose publication use, again, not a primary function of the organisation. By contrast, the professional sector of the market is that in which desktop publishing performs an **essential** function for the organisation or department. For example, if a company is in the business of printing, design or publishing, then its primary function will revolve around (or significantly rely upon) the production of artwork in one form or another. A department in a large organisation, whose responsibility is the publications and printing for the organisation as a whole, would likewise find desktop publishing playing a major role.

The significance of the resource of desktop publishing to an organisation will have an effect on the choice of system employed. As a general rule, electronic publishing systems are sophisticated desktop publishing systems aimed at users who are familiar with printing and publishing.

From the layperson's point of view, the difference between PC-based page make-up systems and electronic publishing may not be obvious at first, or indeed, may never be obvious. So what characteristics help identify electronic publishing from the wider, more general market of applications?

Here are a few pointers:

- they may be as much as twice the price of the most popular middle range packages, ie around £900 or more;
- they support much more sophisticated output devices which will include one or more industry standard phototypesetters;
- they allow much finer control over the page layout – including spacing, positioning and other typographical aspects not essential for general-purpose use but which may be critical for professional typesetting;
- they tend to rely on a coding system, more than a mouse, as a means of assigning style attributes;
- they are less likely to employ the use of an interactive WYSIWYG screen, but rather a preview facility which allows the operator to choose when to view the job in WYSIWYG mode;
- they are better at handling text entry, often providing many standard word processor type facilities;
- they are often sold as a cheaper and more adaptable alternative to conventional phototypesetting 'front ends'.

Each of the above characteristics will now be discussed in more detail.

Price

As one might expect, the better the quality of the software system, the higher the market price. The more specialised a system tends to be, the higher the price will be. Both apply to electronic publishing systems and consequently they are noticeably more expensive across the board than the general-purpose PC-based systems. As a rough guide, the comparisons of the pricing among the various group categories are as follows:

Group I	WP-based DTP	From £60 to £600
Group II	PC-based page make-up	From £70 to £800
Group III	Electronic publishing systems	From £800 to £6,000
Group IV	Dedicated electronic publishing – usually sold as a complete hardware and software solution.	£5,000+

Since electronic publishing systems often have to be able to output to high-quality devices such as phototypesetters (see below), the price may vary according to the system they are to interface with. The term used to refer to the function of the system which controls the output is *device driver.* Like someone who drives a car, thereby controlling what it does, a device driver controls what the output device does. Desktop publishing systems may express their output capabilities in terms of the printers and typesetters they support. The cost of a 'driver' for a phototypesetter may be an additional cost to the standard package which might offer laser printer support as an in-built standard. The cost of phototypesetter drivers on electronic publishing systems can be as much as or more than the cost of the basic software package.

Output Devices

Most desktop publishing software systems, with the exception of the cheapest packages, will provide support for output to a laser printer of one type or another. As Chapter 4 explains further, there are different types of laser printer, but most offer the same degree of resolution (ie the finest degree of smoothness that can be given to the form of a character). Many will also allow output to a standard dot matrix printer, though the quality of the print is much lower.

There is a considerable gap between the resolution of the laser printer and that of phototypesetting, and there is an equally considerable gap between the cost of a laser printer and that of a phototypesetter. Because phototypesetters are so expensive (from around £9,000) they are not so commonly supported as an output device, except in electronic publishing systems, and even then, they tend to be limited to a certain manufacturer. If an organisation has a phototypesetter at all, it will only be interested in a device driver for that particular one anyway.

There are systems that support several phototypesetters, however, in order to offer flexibility to the user who wishes to compose page layouts on a microcomputer at their own desktop, but wants to send the output to a device that is external to the organisation. Some typesetting bureaux, for example, offer a service of processing the output of a desktop publishing system, either by receiving a disk containing the publication's files, or by a communication link using a telephone line.

Layout Control

A skilled and experienced designer employing the use of electronic publishing will want as much typographical control of the page layout as possible. This includes being able to employ facilities for the fine adjustment of spacing between characters, lines and words, being able to adjust the size of a typeface by small increments, allowing the accurate positioning of text blocks, rules and other elements by exact co-ordinates, and so on.

These are features that are given less emphasis in the general use market applications. The reason for this is because the user of the more commonly used PC-based desktop publishing system is not trained in the skills of typesetting. Essentially, the system must be easy to use, and for the most part, this means that the process of manipulation of the text is based upon simple operations, often using the mouse. For example, to place a box around a block of text, the general application software system will achieve this by using the mouse pointing device to 'drag' open a box of a given thickness of line into a position which visually appears to be correct. In other words, the location of the elements relies more upon the eye than on precise measurement. There may be 'rulers' present to help positioning, but they lack the accuracy of specifying the precise co-ordinates of the corners of the box, to locate it in relation to the margins of the page or column.

Such fine control is expected by the professional typesetter who will be used to using such systems if conventional phototypesetting has been employed in the organisation in the past. If electronic publishing is to offer a serious alternative to conventional phototypesetting systems, then this more accurate approach is expected. Equally important is that the operator is expected to be more able to cope with using more precise systems, which might otherwise be daunting to the average office user or secretary simply trying to produce an attractive board report, for example.

Another reason that electronic publishing systems offer finer control over the layout of page elements, is that if a phototypesetter is used as the output device, the very fact that it is itself capable of much finer and more precise output, dictates the degree of control which must be afforded by the software that drives it.

Operator Interface

As previously mentioned, the general-purpose desktop publishing systems nearly all employ the use of a mouse pointing device, and most cannot function efficiently without one. This is not because the process of page make-up itself demands the use of such a device, rather that the screen interface used by page make-up application software, with its pull-down menus and paper-like screen, all of which were copied from the early developments on the Apple computers, need the mouse as a means of operator-screen interface. To choose options, functions, styles, etc from menus, to execute commands, to move page elements around the screen, to highlight and select areas and blocks of text, and to draw and manipulate graphics, the mouse has become the definitive tool for the job. However, the skilled and experienced phototypesetter, the graphic designer, typographer or paste-up artist who has either used conventional phototypesetting systems or no computerised systems at all, will not be used to manipulating page elements in this way.

Despite a move in this direction by most major phototypesetter manufacturers, the use of WYSIWYG and mouse interfaces remains an option rather than an enforced method of computer page make-up. Instead, conventional systems have tended to rely upon a code-based interface. In fact, it is rather like using a more complex and extended version of the 'tagging' of word processor files described previously. In order to choose a particular typeface for a heading, for example, rather than choosing it from a pull-down menu, the text concerned is preceded with a code which defines the typeface to the phototypesetter or laser printer. Hence, the code [FT1] might indicate font number 1 which might happen to be Univers Bold. All other characteristics are similarly defined. Even the width of a column may be defined by a command that specifies the measure of the line (measure being a term for the width or line length) such as [ll26] where 26 is the number of picas width (picas being a measuring unit used in printing and design).

Using such code-based systems looks complicated to a layperson. Instead of selecting choices and styles from a series of menus to define the appearance of a paragraph of text, a code-based system could employ something like this:

> [aj][ft01][ll26][ls11][ps10][ko][ho][il02]This is a sample paragraph defined on a conventional phototypesetting system.

The string of codes in front of the text itself can be positively frightening to a newcomer to desktop publishing, but to the experienced eye, all the following controls have been assigned to the paragraph:

[aj] text automatically justified
[ft01] font table reference 1
[ll26] measure 26 picas
[ls11] leading 11 points
[ps10] point size 10
[ko] kerning on
[ho] hyphenation on
[il02] indent text 2 picas from left margin

There are many electronic publishing systems that employ such coding systems. Some offer the WYSIWYG alternative as an optional interface.

With code-based systems, checking the appearance of the document before it is printed is achieved by using a preview facility. This is a function of the software which allows the operator, at the touch of a key, to display a 'printed out' version of the page on the screen. In other words, the screen pretends to be the output device and displays the document page as though it had been printed out on paper. In essence, this is also a form of WYSIWYG, except that such a display is not interactive, ie it does not remain on screen while text editing is being carried out. Text and commands are entered in a word processing-type screen environment; then the preview is used to occasionally check that the output will be as expected. For the experienced typesetter operator this is often sufficient to check that the page layout is correct.

Using codes also makes the process of fine adjustment that much easier, since every attribute that affects the text has to be individually specified. Therefore, any one of the attributes can be adjusted, usually by very small amounts, and there is usually more flexibility than general-purpose systems provide.

Code-based electronic publishing systems also cater for style sheets and templates. To save keying in a whole string of codes every time a particular style is required, the operator can often assign names to code strings and uses a shortened version, just like the tagging facility used when interfacing word processors to PC-based page make-up systems. In addition, the operator may be able to assign strings of commands to a single keystroke or a combination of two keystrokes. This speeds up the editing process. These are called macros, and are referred to, on conventional typesetting systems, as user-definable keystrokes (UDKs).

Competition for Standard Front Ends

The fact that electronic publishing software (apart from the dedicated systems described below) operate on standard business microcomputers (IBM PCs and the like) means that they are usually a cheaper alternative to a conventional front end system supplied with a phototypesetter. The disadvantage is that a standard microcomputer lacks the special keyboard facilities of a special computer, but apart from that, they are more flexible, as they are suitable for use with other applications, provided, of course, they are not fully employed in the role of page make-up.

With the market for cheaper personal computers flooded with different systems and designs, the choice is wide. With the attachment of accessories, such as paper-size video screens (A4 and A3), the personal computer offers a very competitively priced front end to the typesetter. This is particularly important if the system is to be used by more than one operator. Consider a publications environment where several operators need page make-up facilities, but are all accessing one phototypesetter. The cost of additional terminals on a phototypesetter, using a conventional front end at £5,000 or more, can be excessive compared to the cost of a personal computer at under £2,000.

DEDICATED SYSTEMS

These are systems that bundle the electronic publishing software of the type described above, with special hardware designed specifically for page make-up. The hardware, for example, might incorporate an A4 screen, special keyboard with keys for unusual characters and typesetting commands, and an optional mouse device.

These systems are really just alternatives to the conventional phototypesetting systems, but may employ a laser printer as either the main output device, or for proofing purposes. The advantages of such a system include:

- specialised hardware and software facilities built-in;
- complete system from one supplier, making support and maintenance easier to manage.

Disadvantages include:

- less adaptable to a changing and developing market – all technology tied to one supplier;
- costly for additional terminals compared to PCs;
- often occupies more space than PC-based systems.

4 Technology Developments

With the exception of dedicated systems, the hardware associated with desktop publishing is not unique to this application. The machines used are often standard personal computers and there is a wide choice of publishing software packages to suit almost every microcomputer – for home, business and academic use. The rapid development of the desktop publishing market has, however, brought about the exploitation of existing hardware for desktop publishing use, to the extent that it is common for those who are unfamiliar with the background to desktop publishing to think of the associated technology as completely new.

COMPUTERS

For almost every microcomputer on the market, there is a desktop publishing software package available, but by far the most widely catered for is the IBM personal computer and any compatible machines by other manufacturers. The IBM PC format, in whatever model, remains the most widely used and recognised format of microcomputer, though possibly in the field of desktop publishing it has one very significant rival – the Apple Macintosh.

The Macintosh was the forerunner of all desktop publishing computers because of its, then, unique method of screen display and operator interface. It already had the 'paper white' screen, with black text on a white background like a sheet of printed paper, which made it ideal for WYSIWYG displays in publishing applications. By contrast, almost all other general-use microcomputers had screens with black backgrounds and bright green text, or were based on colour monitors. Early word processing software developed on the Macintosh, together with the choice of typefaces and styles that could be seen on the screen in the size and style they would be printed, made it the obvious choice for early desktop publishing development. The advantage that this gave to the Apple publishing applications remains with it today, though the IBM computer was soon to follow in the footsteps of Apple and offer screen interfaces that mimicked those of the Macintosh. One of the most popular general-use desktop publishing software packages on the market today, called PageMaker, was first developed for distribution on the Apple Macintosh. Later it was released for use on the IBM and compatible computers, making it one of the most widely selected software solutions for page make-up. Its rival software package, Ventura, which is marketed by Xerox remained available only on Xerox and IBM-compatible machines and has never been developed for the Macintosh.

The choice of microcomputer most suitable for desktop publishing may largely depend on its ability to integrate with existing systems. The disk and file storage formats of Apple microcomputers are not directly compatible with IBM computers. If an organisation which uses IBM compatibles for word processing wishes to acquire a page make-up system, it is likely that an IBM compatible will be chosen as the host microcomputer. A text file stored on a disk from an IBM machine cannot be placed in the disk drive of an Apple Macintosh and read by Apple software. However, if the Apple Macintosh seems the most favourable machine for other reasons, ie because of the available software, then there are other ways of getting information from one type of machine to the other.

For example, for the Apple Macintosh, there is an external disk drive option which will read IBM format diskettes, so that information can be passed between IBM and Apple software applications. An alternative link can be provided by a communications cable connected to both computers, and a software program controls the passing of data from one machine to another.

With the possible exception of PageMaker, which is available on both IBM and Apple computers, the choice of microcomputer should most often be made on the basis of the software available. It is the software, not the hardware, that will determine what desktop publishing facilities are available. Attention should also be given to word processors, as these may be used as the principal means of text input. Having found the right software, the hardware is largely secondary — again, apart from the consideration of integration with any existing computers in the organisation.

Desktop publishing systems consume large amounts of computer memory. To run the most popular and comprehensive software packages, microcomputers need large amounts of processing memory or RAM. In addition, the file storage requirements of publications that have been formatted on a desktop publishing system will require more disk space than the equivalent text stored in a word processor file. Graphics, too, take up large amounts of disk space, even for one picture. Because of this, many standard microcomputers require enhancements to make additional working memory available, if they are to comfortably handle the running of the software. Machines like the Apple Macintosh have large amounts of memory, at least 1 Mbyte, built in as standard. They also have fast and powerful processing capabilities, and both these factors make them ideal for desktop publishing. They cost more, however, even as a basic model, compared to IBM PCs, so you get what you pay for.

For the IBM and compatible machines, there may often be a need to upgrade the standard model to make it suitable for desktop publishing. For example:

- additional memory (RAM) can be added if the existing memory proves to be inadequate;

- graphics cards (circuit boards) may need to be added if the computer's screen is not capable of coping with the display of non-text characters;

- high-resolution screen displays are required, if the monitor of the standard machine cannot display a sharp enough image to make page make-up display possible;

- additional disk storage capacity is necessary if the standard machine does not offer sufficient disk space to hold the programs and the associated data files.

To find out what is needed, you have to check with the supplier of the software, or the sales literature of the desktop publishing software package that you intend to use, to ensure that the microcomputer is capable of running the software comfortably. A word of warning, however, with regards to 'minimum requirements' – these are the minimum hardware facilities needed to operate the software and are often stated on literature and documentation associated with the software. These state what simplest configuration will enable the software to operate, but this may not be the best configuration for acceptable performance. If memory is short, for example, the software will make continual reference to the disk storage device of the machine in order to load instructions into memory – swapping one set of instructions for another as you make changes on the screen or select specific functions. This can make the operation of the software tediously slow, and more memory in the machine may avoid this.

MOUSE

For systems that offer a WYSIWYG approach, the mouse is the means by which a cursor is moved around the display area of a page layout, and by which text, graphics and other elements are selected, positioned and manipulated on the screen. Some popular microcomputers now come with a mouse as standard, but for others one can be acquired for as little as £50.

There are two types of mechanism that determine how the mouse translates movement on a desktop to that of the cursor on the screen. Mechanical mice use a large, rubber-coated ball bearing. When the ball is rolled along the surface of the desk, or even in your hand, the rotation of the ball moves rollers which make contact with the ball's surface and these are translated into co-ordinates. The other type of mechanism is optical. This uses a grid pad on the desktop, which is read by an optical device in the base of the mouse to translate into co-ordinates affecting the position of the cursor on the screen. The disadvantage of optical mice is that they require the special pad on which to operate, which uses up more of your desk space.

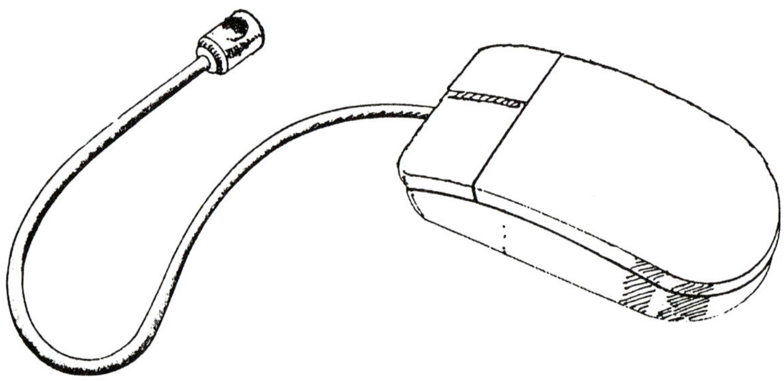

Figure 4.1 Mouse

You may see pads for sale for mechanical mice. These should not be confused with the special surface required by an optical mouse. Pads for mechanical mice are simply special surfaces which facilitate the rolling of the ball, helping it to grip and improving the response and accuracy compared to its performance on a shiny desk surface. They also help protect the desk surface from being scratched, but they are not essential for the operation of the device.

MONITORS

Standard microcomputer monitors or screens, whether colour or monochrome, can be quite adequate for most desktop publishing software packages, but for users who are considering desktop publishing as the primary use for the computer, a larger screen size can be most beneficial as it improves the viewing area of the page layouts. For desktop publishing software that uses the interactive display or preview method of showing the page layout, a popular choice of monitor is one with an A4 or A3 sized screen, both of which can show a full A4 page with good clarity. This saves having to move up and down the page to see the top half, then the bottom half, or having to zoom the display until the page is scaled down to fit the screen – the kind of manoeuvres necessary when using a standard 25-line monitor.

When page views are scaled down they are difficult to read, and are therefore generally only suitable when viewing the overall arrangement of the text and graphics elements of a page. For standard screens, working on the text has usually to be done while viewing only part of the page; otherwise the text would be unreadable. Most of the dedicated microcomputers for desktop publishing are fitted with the larger screen sizes, and for standard microcomputer users, A4 and A3 screens are available as optional extras. They do not have to be made by the same manufacturer as the original microcomputer, so long as they are compatible with it, so you may need to check first before purchasing one.

Page make-up systems that use a WYSIWYG screen display recreate a representation of black text on white paper, and all text and graphics are shown as if they were printed on paper. Even with 'green screen' monitors, some desktop publishing software systems reverse the display so that the background is green and the text black. Because of this style of presentation, microcomputers that have a colour monitor tend to be preferred to the green screen ones, because they can provide a bright white paper-like background. Some software packages allow different text styles to be shown in different colours too, so this favours the colour monitor even further.

Monitor resolution can vary from one computer to another. Resolution has to do with how fine the detail on the screen can be displayed and is measured in dots per square inch. The higher the resolution, the sharper the image on the screen and the finer the detail is shown. Word processors are suitable for any resolution of screen because they do not normally display the text in the style it will be printed. However, a desktop publishing system, when showing a preview or interactive page display, attempts to recreate the typeface, type size and graphics as closely as possible to the way in which it will eventually be printed. Since a typeface of a small size can be difficult to represent if the resolution of the monitor is low, high-resolution monitors are favoured.

Another component of the computer which affects the display is the graphics card. This is a circuit board which plugs inside the computer and controls the display of graphics on the monitor.

Most desktop publishing systems will support more than one class of monitor and/or graphics card. When checking through the system requirements list of a package, terms that you are likely to encounter, with respect to the display, include the following:

EGA	(enhanced graphics adaptor)
VGA	(video graphics array)
CGA	(colour graphics adaptor)
Mono	(monochrome monitor)

Hercules graphics adaptor

The resolution of the monitors is shown as a pair of numbers which represent the number of picture elements in the screen area, eg 640 x 350 or 640 x 480.

The resolution of the monitor has no bearing on the quality of the output, since the resolution of the printer may be, and usually is, quite different. The preference for a high-resolution screen is simply to assist the operator by offering a sharper picture, which is particularly useful when manipulating graphic images.

KEYBOARDS

For standard microcomputers, the keyboard usually comprises the following sections of keytops:

- a standard qwerty set, as used on all keyboard devices, originating from the typewriter keyboard layout;
- a numerics keypad, like that of a calculator;
- four directional arrow keys, used to move the cursor on the screen; hence their name of cursor control keys.

In addition to the above, the keyboard may include a few function keys. These are keys that carry out a special function, and that will depend upon the software being used at the time. The number of function keys vary. Some have special names such as escape, home, page up, etc; others simply a number like F1, F2, F3, etc. On many business microcomputers, between 10 and 12 numbered function keys are provided. When the computer is being used for desktop publishing, the software may make use of these keys to allow certain functions or options to be engaged which short cut making a selection from, say, a pull-down menu or typing in a lengthy command. For example, pressing the function key F6 may cause any selected text to adopt a bold typestyle. Similarly, F7 might select italics. Some software packages will let you assign whole styles or paragraph tags to function keys of your own choice. This enables text to be selected and then adopt all the characteristics of a predefined tag, such as a bold, centred, 14-point Helvetica heading.

For general-purpose desktop publishing systems, the use of a standard microcomputer keyboard is sufficient to cope with the various functions. However, the more comprehensive the software, particularly with electronic publishing, the more specialised the various keystrokes may need to be.

Dedicated systems and conventional phototypesetting system keyboards have many additional keytops compared to that of a standard microcomputer. Even special characters are given keys of their own, like accepted letters or symbols such as copyright signs © and registration marks ®.

The professional operator needs to be able to control the keyboard with speed. In an organisation whose business is typesetting or page design, keyboard time is precious and needs to be accurate. Using a single key on a specialised keyboard may be the equivalent of a combination of two or three keystrokes on a standard microcomputer keyboard.

SCANNERS

A scanner is a piece of equipment used to transfer images into a form usable by desktop publishing software, so that they can be printed out, either directly or within a page layout, or transmitted like a facsimile document. Scanning devices are able to cope with graphics images that have already been produced by some other means. A typical example is a black and white photograph which needs to be incorporated into a page of text and printed out with the whole document. Without the scanning facility, the photographs would have to be pasted onto the document after the rest of the page was printed; but, having been scanned, the photographic image is converted into one made up of a series of dots. Once converted in this way, the image can be stored on a disk in electronic form, in what is called a graphics or picture file.

Figure 4.2 Scanned Photograph

Many desktop publishing systems provide the means to recognise graphics files so that a picture may be incorporated into the document, and scanners provide the means to convert the original picture. Once printed graphics are scanned, you can then use the computer to edit the picture or merge it with other graphics. The cost of a desktop scanning device can be around £1,000, though they are getting cheaper, and you can get a hand-held scanner for as little as £200 to £300.

Some scanners are suitable for copying text as well as graphics. By using a scanner which is capable of optical character recognition, text that has been previously printed out can be input into a word processor or desktop publishing package without being retyped.

The quality of the scanned image when printed out will depend entirely upon the capabilities of the output device attached to your computer. A scanned image will not be as detailed as a screened photograph which is pasted onto the artwork afterwards. For this reason, publications that require high-quality reproduction of photographic images will not find a scanner suitable unless it is a very expensive professional system used in conjunction with a phototypesetter.

OUTPUT DEVICES

These are the printers and typesetters on which the actual pages from a desktop publishing system are output. They generally fall into one of three categories:

- dot matrix printer costing from under £100 to about £1,000;
- laser printer costing from about £800 to £18,000;
- phototypesetter costing from about £9,000 to about £100,000.

PHOTOTYPESETTERS

A phototypesetter is a system that uses photosensitive paper, on which an image of the page is projected in one of three ways:

- by a laser beam of light;
- the image of a cathode ray tube (like a small television set);
- by shining light through a kind of stencil.

Phototypesetters are capable of producing the highest quality of all output, but are very expensive compared to printers. They usually require an additional processing device to process the image on the paper, using small tanks of developing chemical similar to that used in photographic print processes. For most requirements, the use of a phototypesetter as an output device is much too expensive, unless the application of desktop publishing is an essential part of the business.

However, the fact that many systems can communicate with such devices does open up the possibilities of using the facilities of a phototypesetter at a remote site for those occasional documents that demand the highest quality output. Many typesetting bureaux offer a service to users of desktop publishing systems whereby they receive prepared documents on disk in a format suitable for output on their particular phototypesetting device, and then send back the typeset output, usually charging on the basis of the number of pages or characters processed.

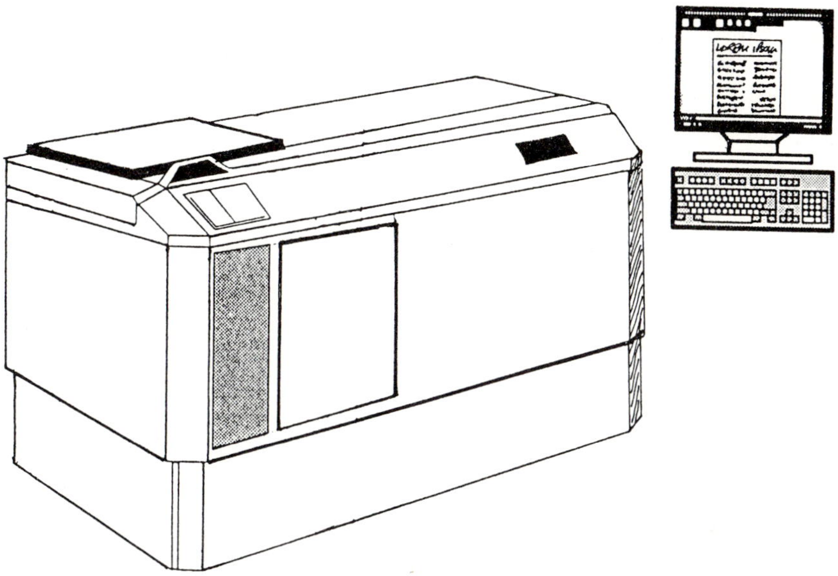

Figure 4.3 Phototypesetter

LASER PRINTERS

The next step down in output quality is that provided by laser printers. For most purposes the laser printer offers an acceptably high quality for most publishing requirements, including graphics. The technology on which they are based is not far removed from that of a dry paper photocopier. They take the paper from paper trays, onto which an image is produced using toner which is heat sealed for permanence – just like with a photocopier. The difference between a laser printer and a photocopier is that the source of the image for a photocopier is another piece of printed matter, whereas the laser printer reproduces an image using instructions from the computer to which it is attached.

Laser printers are quite expensive and, like all other computer devices, vary so much in price. At the time of writing, laser printers are available for just under £900, but some can cost £3,000 or more. Laser printers vary in speed just like other printers, but rather than being measured in number of characters printed per second, they are measured in number of pages printed per minute. This is because laser printers are, in fact, page printers – the whole page being printed in one go.

The standard speeds of laser printer at the time of publication are as follows:

6 pages per minute
8 pages per minute (most common speed)
12 pages per minute
26 pages per minute

The faster the printer, the more expensive. Other factors which affect the price of laser printers include: the paper holding facilities (some can hold large amounts of paper in more than one paper tray); the size of paper that can be handled (most cannot handle anything bigger than A4, but there are some that cope with A3); and the resolution of the printer.

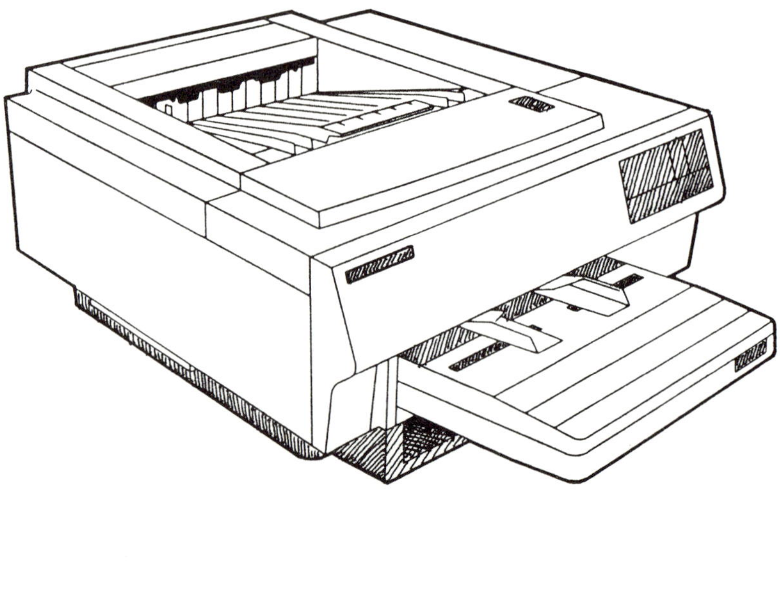

Figure 4.4 Laser Printer

There are two main categories of laser printer and these are described below:

PCL PRINTERS

PCL stands for printer command language. Laser printers that operate by this method employ a process which involves the printer receiving sets of codes that determine how the output is to appear. If the text is to change size or style, for example, the printer must receive an appropriate code sequence to tell it what to do. These sets of codes are usually unique to the printer design, and the most commonly used PCL is that of the Hewlett Packard LaserJet. This is an industry-standard laser printer which many similar laser printers from other manufacturers emulate.

You may come across the term HP LaserJet emulation in sales literature and advertisements for laser printers. It is an indication that the laser printer uses a PCL method of controlling output.

PCL printers are commonly used where standard office documents are the main application of the desktop publishing system. Where more complex publishing is required, the second type of printer, described in the next section, is favoured.

These types of laser printer can produce different typefaces in one of three ways:

- by using information about a typeface already held in the printer's own memory (called resident fonts);
- by extending the known typefaces by plugging in a cartridge;
- by receiving information, from the software package on the connected computer, about a typeface before the printer uses it (called downloadable or soft fonts).

POSTSCRIPT/PDL PRINTERS

PostScript is one of the most widely used terms which is specific to desktop publishing. PostScript is, in fact, a trade name of a company called Adobe Systems Inc, but is commonly misused. PostScript is often used as a generic term for what is in fact a page description language (PDL).

Laser printers that use a page description language to control the output are often referred to as PostScript printers and they have specific advantages over the PCL printers described previously.

A page description language is a software program. It may be 'resident' inside the printer itself, supplied on a circuit board that slots inside the computer, or part of an application software package running on the computer, perhaps as part of the page make-up software.

It controls the output of the printer by describing the complete layout of the page, including all elements of text, graphics, etc. In other words, the whole page is processed in one go. Hence the term 'page printers' is often used to describe laser printers. The advantage of this is that by building up an image of the entire page as a whole pattern of dots, where graphics are not treated any differently than text, you have greater control over the output.

PostScript has become the industry standard page description language, and while there are others available, almost all desktop publishing systems provide PostScript controlled output as an option. In some electronic publishing systems, PostScript may be the only method of producing output.

CHOOSING BETWEEN PCL AND POSTSCRIPT

Faced with a choice between a PCL and a PostScript laser printer, the first thing that will be noticeably different is the price tag. PostScript-compatible printers are, on average, about £1,000 more expensive than PCL printers. The price of a PCL printer will start at about £800, while PostScript printers start at around £2,500.

It is important, therefore, to understand the differences and to establish whether, for your organisation, a PostScript printer is really necessary.

Advantages of PostScript Printers

1) Page description languages are very flexible. The language itself is not specific to any particular device. Rather, devices are made so that they can interpret the PostScript language. This means PostScript can be used to control a phototypesetter as well as a laser printer, without the need for changing the instructions associated with the format of the original document.

   If a publication is produced on a page make-up system that supports the output in PostScript language, the same document can be printed on both a PostScript laser printer and a PostScript phototypesetter without further intervention. In such circumstances, laser printers may be used as proofing devices for what will ultimately be produced on a phototypesetter.

2) PostScript laser printers offer much more variety of typefaces and sizes than do PCL printers. The PostScript language enables typeface information to be programmed by software running on the computer, but most PostScript laser printers have many built-in typefaces, including the currently standard 35 typefaces shown below:

Helvetica	Franklin Gothic

Times	Friz Quadrata
Courier	ITC Galliard
Symbol	ITC Garamond
ITC Avant Garde	Glypha
ITC Bookman	Goudy
Trump Mediaeval	Orator
Palatino	Park Avenue
Century Schoolbook	Prestige Elite
Zapf Chancery	Sonata
Zapf Dingbats	ITC Souvenir
American Typewriter	ITC Korinna
ITC Benguiat	Letter Gothic
Bodoni	Lubalin Graph
Bodoni Poster	ITC Machine
Century Old Style	Melior
Cheltenham	Optima
New Baskerville	

3) Due to the way in which PostScript describes the output of a whole page made up of tiny dots, rather than describing single characters individually, there is greater flexibility over the sizing and scaling of output. For all typefaces offered, PostScript printers allow very small increments in type size (perhaps as little as a quarter-of-a-point increments – see glossary for point sizes).

Not only can the operator control the type sizes in this way, but whether printing graphics, text or both, the entire page can be zoomed, at the time of printing, to a different output size than that of the original document. For example, from 200% actual size down to 1% in 1% increments. No standard PCL printer can do this.

4) PostScript laser printers can cope with certain visual effects not available on standard PCL printers; for example, reverse video (white text on a black background).

5) The graphics handling abilities and the quality of graphics output from PostScript printers is usually superior to PCL printers.

6) Many accessories, such as scanners, produce PostScript files of the images that they reproduce.

7) They usually have large amounts of built-in memory, essential for producing complex documents and graphics.

Disadvantages of PostScript Printers

1) They are more expensive that PCL laser printers.

2) If the laser printer is to be used for printing output from other applications (apart from desktop publishing) such as business accounting software or spreadsheets, a PostScript printer may not be supported, and only some of the PostScript printers are able to emulate industry standard dot matrix printers as a built-in option.

Advantages of PCL Printers

1) They are the cheapest type of laser printer.

2) They offer adequate output control for most office documentation and can be independently controlled by software to produce high quality and complex images.

3) They are often capable of emulating many industry standard dot matrix printers, such as Epson FX and IBM Graphics, as a built-in option.

4) They can subsequently be upgraded to PostScript compatibility, as an option, making them useful as a low-cost entry into desktop publishing with an option to extend later.

5) For some professional electronic publishing systems that use their own language to control document layout and multiple typeface output, PCL printers may be all that is required, making PostScript an unnecessary additional expense.

Disadvantages of PCL Printers

1) Fewer typefaces (fonts) are built-in. There may only be Courier 12 point normal and bold, which is no more than a single daisywheel would offer, and as this is not a proportional typeface it is unsuitable for anything other than normal business correspondence and reports. Others may offer additional typefaces built-in:

Swiss	(similar to Helvetica)
Dutch	(similar to Times)

Additional typefaces have to be supplied in one of two ways:

- Plug-in cartridges that fit into the printer and supply the necessary information for additional typefaces, though each cartridge may only offer another two typefaces;

- Downloadable or soft fonts – these are sent to the printer by the software on the computer. They describe the typeface information for a given piece of text and are processed using the PCL printer's spare memory. This may require more memory than the standard PCL printer can offer, so additional memory may need to be provided to use them. Soft fonts are slower to process than internal fonts, and may require considerable disk space to store them ready for use.

These additional typefaces are, of course, a supplementary expense to the basic printer, though they are available from a choice of independent suppliers from as little as £20 per font.

2) Type sizes are usually restricted to specific sizes unless downloadable/soft fonts are used. For example, a font cartridge may offer the following typefaces and sizes:

Helvetica Bold	14 point
Times Roman Medium	10 point
Times Roman Bold	10 point
Times Medium Italic	10 point
Times Roman Medium	8 point
Lineprinter Medium	8.5 point

Compared to the choice of built-in type sizes of a PostScript printer, offering anything from 4 point to 127 point for any of 35 typefaces, this is severely limited.

3) The cost to upgrade to PostScript compatibility may be as much as the cost of the original printer, ultimately making it no cheaper than buying PostScript in the first place.

4) PCL language is not used by phototypesetters, so a document produced for output on a PCL printer will need re-formatting for output on a different device.

5) PCL printers often come with insufficient built-in memory to handle complex graphics. Therefore additional memory may need to be purchased in order to process half-tone images or more than a few typefaces on the same page.

Final Decision

Looking at the above advantages and disadvantages, you might wonder why anyone chooses a PCL printer. Yet PCL printers of the Hewlett Packard LaserJet variety remain one of the most popular and widely sold laser printers on the market. It all depends on what you want to achieve and what your budget is. It also depends on the type of software you are using. There are some professional electronic publishing software systems that do not need PostScript to provide multiple typefaces and fine output control of both text and graphics. Such systems use their own 'language', which works beneath the basic PCL language to drive the engine of the laser printer, offering considerably more control than the basic printer normally provides. In addition, you can acquire software alternatives to PostScript for use with PCL printers. One example is a package called GoScript, which enables PostScript output to be produced on a PCL printer, such as the HP LaserJet, together with many typeface choices, and is entirely software controlled so that there is no need for additional hardware. At a cost of around £200, it provides a serious alternative to PostScript laser printers.

As far as output quality is concerned, it is generally only in the area of graphics that PostScript devices have an advantage. Apart from that, PCL printers are adequate for many publication jobs. This book, for example, was typeset on the Hewlett Packard LaserJet Series II PCL printer.

DOT MATRIX PRINTERS

Dot matrix printers are among the cheapest printers you can buy. They are not complicated mechanically and are generally very reliable.

Dot matrix printers can print at different speeds. When used for printing out listings from computers, where the quality of type is not a high priority, some dot matrix printers can output at the rate of 500 characters per second or more. Compare this to the 40 characters per second, or thereabouts, of a daisywheel printer. Draft printing, as it is known, is when a dot matrix printer produces characters using the minimum number of dots to make them readable, sacrificing quality for speed. The higher the quality required for the printed character, the slower the dot matrix printer operates.

Using dot matrix printers may be adequate for introducing the facilities of desktop publishing, but for most quality applications an organisation will need to consider acquiring a laser printer.

UNSUITABLE PRINTERS

Printers not suitable for desktop publishing include any daisywheel printers, or electronic typewriters that can be used as printers when connected to a computer. This is because they cannot reproduce any type styles or typefaces other than the one type and size on the daisywheel itself, and few can offer any graphics characters.

RESOLUTION

All output printers mentioned in association with desktop publishing produce anything from characters with different styles of letters and numbers to whole images, or a mixture of both, by simply placing dots on the paper. The finer the dots, and the more dots that can be printed in a given area, the finer the quality of the result. This is what is measured by the 'resolution' of the printer. A printer that cannot produce many fine dots in a given area is said to be a low-resolution printer. One that can produce many is called a high-resolution printer.

The resolution of any digital device that prints using dots is measured in dots per inch. The unit of measurement is often written as dpi. So, if a printer can print 100 dots per inch of space, its resolution would be written as 100 dpi. In many cases, this measurement actually reflects the dots per square inch. In other words, if a printer can produce 100 dots per horizontal inch, then it can usually do the same in a vertical inch. Strictly, then, the resolution could be described as, say, 100 x 100 dpi, which is 10,000 dots per square inch. Not all devices work like this, however – there are some printers that have a higher resolution in one direction than in another.

For the purposes of high-quality desktop publishing output, the following resolutions are currently standard:

300 dpi - almost all popular laser printers
400 dpi - now available on a few laser printers
600 dpi - available on very few laser printers but at a cost which makes them uncompetitive with phototypesetting

1,200 dpi - typical resolutions of
2,400 dpi phototypesetting systems

From this it can be seen that the resolution of phototypesetters is considerably higher, yet laser printers remain the most common output device for desktop publishing at present.

As stated above, 300 dpi is the most common resolution for laser printers. Higher-resolution laser printing does create more complex technical problems for the manufacturers than may be expected. The step from a resolution of 300 dpi (90,000 dots per square inch) to 400 dpi (160,000 dots per square inch) requires an improvement of one third. Added to this, the laser beam itself has to be more accurate, and the paper transport must be steadier.

5 Applications

Desktop publishing is a very popular software application. It is easy to demonstrate to potential users because most people can understand this use of the technology. We encounter printed material every day of our lives. When we see words and pictures on a computer screen, which represent what will ultimately be a printed document, most of us can understand the basic purpose of the system.

To what use any individual or organisation may put a desktop publishing system may not come immediately to mind. One thinks of the various printed documents, reports and brochures that pass through our hands and presume that desktop publishing systems have some part to play. Broadly speaking, the application of desktop publishing is in almost any area that involves print and design. However, the specific purpose for which it is used can vary considerably. For one job, desktop publishing may provide the means to produce an entire publication, from conception to the finished document, yet in another case, desktop publishing may only assist in providing one aspect of the artwork, one component, if you like, of the complete publication. All will depend upon the quantity and quality of the job required. If the printing requirement for a particular publication is a complex, full-colour catalogue, which includes many photographic elements, the application of desktop publishing may be quite limited. On the other hand, if the publication is a simple contract report, including a few graphs and charts, the system may be capable of handling the entire publication with ease.

The following paragraphs describe a few common applications, which may give ideas about uses perhaps not already considered. There is no order of preference given to the applications selected, nor any intended implication of suitability of a particular desktop publishing system for any specific purpose mentioned.

CORRESPONDENCE

Letters and circulars, mailshots and reminders can be given an authoritative appearance by the application of desktop publishing. Using a proportional typeface, together with bold headings, or italics to emphasise points of interest, can all help to give correspondence items a more interesting appearance. Most laser printers, by virtue of the fact that they process plain paper, like a photocopier, will allow you to print directly onto business or headed stationery. Beware of headed paper with thermographic logos and addresses (these are raised glossy characters, heat sealed onto the paper) since they have a tendency to melt on the hot rollers of the laser printer and make something of a mess. For a mailshot, using a laser printer to reproduce many copies of a letter may be an attractive idea, though if the numbers to be sent are high (perhaps 1,000 or more) you may possibly stretch the capabilities of the laser printer if this is done on a regular basis. Remember, also, that because a laser printed letter has the appearance of a printed circular, rather than an individually typed document, the effect can seem impersonal.

REPORTS

For internal reports, one might consider the use of desktop publishing to be extravagant. Indeed, if the facility is being used as a toy to impress other members of the organisation, then this is clearly not the correct application of the technology. However, when one considers that the purpose of a report is to convey important information, then any device which enables the meaning to be conveyed more clearly, is worth considering. In particular, the ability of most page make-up systems to permit the integration of graphics within the document, offers the author of the report the opportunity of enhancing the message contained within by the use of illustrations (see Figure 5.1).

Attractive reports are more inviting to read. Complex and lengthy reports often need assistance if they are to receive any degree of attention from recipients within an organisation, and a good page layout, with important key points clearly highlighted, can improve the chances of the message being received and understood. If type sizes are considered appropriately, the overall length of a typeset document can be considerably less than a typed equivalent, and therefore seem a less daunting task to read (assuming that the other extreme is avoided, such that the reader requires a magnifying glass to accompany the report).

Reports that are to be made public, or intended for reading by a client or customer, probably deserve more attention to appearance. Any documentation which is for readership outside the organisation carries with it, either consciously or unconsciously, the image and impression of the organisation itself. For this reason, organisations take

ACME MARKETING INC

Sales Report
Fourth quarter results

The summer sales promotion activity resulted in a **dramatic impact on the uptake of the new product range**, with forward orders increasing rapidly after the first month of promotion. Compared to the previous quarter, the **sales against budget have increased**, and this has had the effect of taking the moving annual turnover total over the budget for this year. However, as a result of the pressures on production to meet the new demand, the take up of short term staff has affected the profit margin, since the casual labour has been more expensive to employ pro-rata than the full time workers (because of shift work). This has therefore increased the cost of sales which has not been adjusted for in prices. The increase in profits for this quarter, then, is at a lower proportion to turnover.

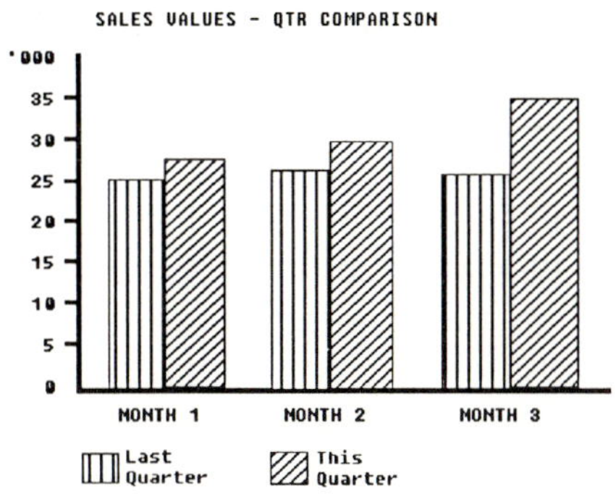

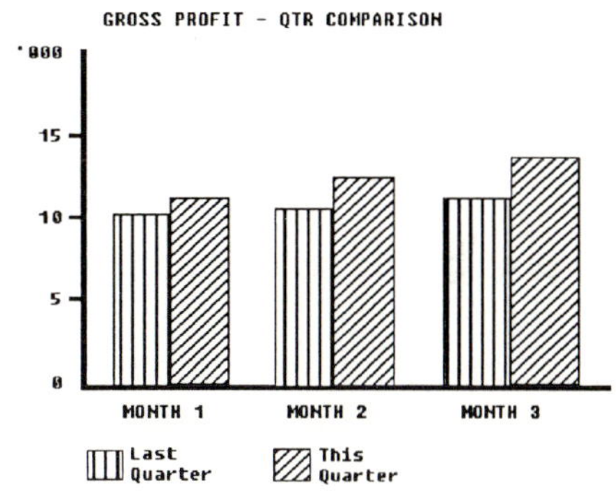

The impact on the gross profit percentage has been to reduce the margin by some 3%. It is expected that the net profit will have been reduced further by the increased use of non-material resources, such as additional canteen facilities and industrial clothing purchases, not adjusted for in the selling price.

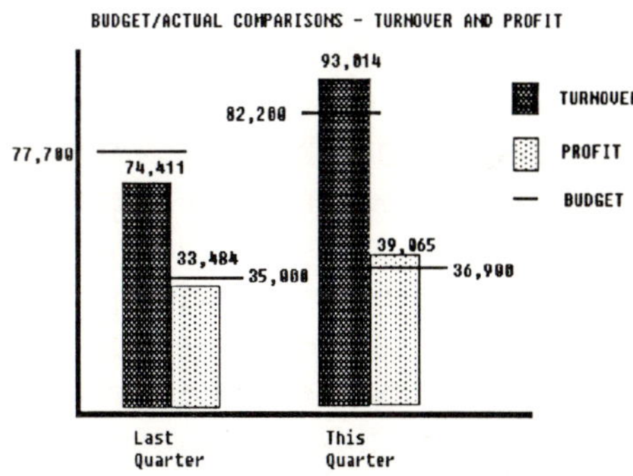

It has been suggested that a meeting is arranged between the production and materials control departments to investigate the possibilities for reducing the profit fall back.

JAD/PD
14th December 1989

Figure 5.1 Report Produced With DTP

the trouble to ensure that their commercial literature is of a high standard. A company preparing a proposal or tender document to a potential client as a one-off document is unlikely to employ the services of designers and printers to enhance the document's appearance. In most cases, the best effort will be made to type a neat document, perhaps bound in a presentable form to add a touch of authority. With the use of desktop publishing, the organisation has a true alternative, and can produce a high-quality example of documentation for the proposal or tender, with typeset text, graphics and illustrations at a fraction of the cost that would be incurred by employing professional services. This is a good application example of desktop publishing in a business environment.

PRICE LISTS, ETC

Price lists, product and service leaflets and the like are examples of documents that may be subject to change with reasonable frequency. This fact may affect the magnitude of expenditure on the quality of the document. One may often see or receive a high-quality colour catalogue accompanied by a typed, photocopied price list inserted separately. It is clear that the prices are subject to change more frequently than the items contained within the catalogue, and the organisation responsible for the publication clearly considered that the cost of printing the price list to the same standard was an unnecessary expense.

The reason for adopting a high-quality approach to the catalogue may have been to convey a good image to the public, and the quality of the price list may be letting it down. The use of desktop publishing to produce a better-quality document, which gives the appearance of being printed, may help the image in this respect. Even if the laser printer is used to produce a good quality master for photocopying, provided the quality of the photocopying is itself acceptable, the result can be a better-looking publication than the typed alternative. As mentioned in the paragraph on reports, using carefully selected type sizes can save on space, and a price list that might otherwise have occupied two or three separate sheets may be condensed into a single leaf and still be perfectly legible. In consequence, a cost reduction can be seen by reducing the amount of paper and processing involved.

NEWSLETTERS

Newsletters and newspaper-style publications are commonly used for either internal readership within an organisation, or as a vehicle for communicating the activities of an organisation to the outside world. They often take the form of a small magazine or newspaper style publication, using two or three columns of text on a page, and including banner style headings across columns, pictures, boxes and rules. All of these elements of a page layout are ideal fodder for desktop publishing systems. Few word processors can offer a multiple-column page layout, but almost every page make-up system, from the cheapest upwards, can provide the multiple-column presentation familiar to most of us in magazines and newspapers.

Many large organisations consider an internal newsletter an ideal way of circulating details of activities, both organisational, social and personal among the employed staff. Using a desktop publishing system to produce such a newsletter is a very attractive application, and one which can be easily handled by most systems. If the numbers are not too high, the laser printer can be employed to produce the required number of copies of the document, which can then be folded or stapled to form an interesting publication that will be more acceptable than a dull-looking typed document which resembles an internal report or memorandum. Such an application of desktop publishing may rarely be considered as a primary reason for acquisition, but it can be a positive benefit on the side.

Newsletters sent to customers and clients or other readers external to the organisation will need to be produced to a reasonably high standard. Desktop publishing systems are well able to handle the layout requirements of such publications, and with the added ability to incorporate scanned photographs in the document, the whole process can be cost-effectively handled internally. Such projects can be costly to run when using outside resources, particularly if quantities are low. Since such documents cannot be directly related to increasing the profitability of an organisation (even though they may possibly be considered as doing so indirectly), they are an expense, and desktop publishing may be used to reduce the costs in this area. Organisations that are non-profit making and have to be very cost conscious, such as charities, educational establishments and local authorities, often have the need to publish reports and news information about the organisation's activities to a wide readership. Where desktop publishing can help is by reducing the cost of specialised services to produce the artwork, eliminating some of the proofing cycles and reducing the overall production timescale. All of these may be a cost benefit.

BOOK PUBLISHING

The use of electronic publishing systems as cost-effective front ends to phototypesetters has enabled book publishers to expand the typesetting facilities, or even consider handling typesetting internally for the first time and thereby reduce the overall production cost. For authors using word processors, the publisher may have a much easier route to typesetting, direct from a disk containing text files. Since most desktop publishing systems operate on standard microcomputers, the author's word processing files are much more likely to be compatible. Previously, the use of multiple disk readers was necessary to convert a word processor disk format to one that could be used by the phototypesetting system.

The cost of typesetting a book can be reduced even further if the

Company Name **Month 00,0000**

Report Title

Subhead 1

By Author Name

Lorem ipsum dolor sit amet, consectetuer adipiscing elit, sed diam nonummy nibh euismod tincidunt ut laoreet dolore magna aliquam erat volutpat. Ut wisi enim ad minim veniam, quis nostrud exerci tation ullamcorper suscipit lobortis nisl ut aliquip ex ea commodo consequat.

Duis autem vel eum iriure dolor in hendrerit in vulputate velit esse molestie consequat, vel illum dolore eu feugiat nulla facilisis at vero eros et accumsan et iusto odio dignissim qui blandit praesent luptatum zzril delenit augue duis dolore te feugait nulla facilisi.

Lorem ipsum dolor sit amet, consectetuer adipiscing elit, sed diam nonummy nibh euismod tincidunt ut laoreet dolore magna aliquam erat volutpat. Ut wisi enim ad minim veniam, quis nostrud exerci tation ullamcorper suscipit lobortis nisl ut aliquip ex ea commodo consequat. Duis autem vel eum iriure dolor in hendrerit in vulputate velit esse molestie consequat, vel illum dolore eu feugiat nulla facilisis at vero eros et accumsan et iusto odio dignissim qui blandit praesent luptatum zzril delenit augue duis dolore te feugait nulla facilisi.

Nam liber tempor cum soluta nobis eleifend option congue nihil imperdiet doming id quod mazim placerat facer possim assum. Lorem ipsum dolor sit amet, consectetuer adipiscing elit, sed diam nonummy nibh euismod tincidunt ut laoreet dolore magna aliquam erat volutpat. Ut wisi enim ad minim veniam, quis nostrud exerci tation ullamcorper suscipit lobortis nisl ut aliquip ex ea commodo consequat.

Duis autem vel eum iriure dolor in hendrerit in vulputate velit esse molestie consequat, vel illum dolore eu feugiat nulla facilisis at vero eros et accumsan et iusto odio dignissim qui blandit praesent luptatum zzril delenit augue duis dolore te feugait nulla facilisi. Lorem ipsum dolor sit amet, consectetuer adipiscing elit, sed diam nonummy nibh euismod tincidunt ut laoreet dolore magna aliquam erat volutpat. Ut wisi enim ad minim veniam, quis nostrud exerci tation ullamcorper suscipit lobortis nisl ut aliquip ex ea commodo consequat. Dui autem vel eum iriure dolor in hendrerit in vulputate velit esse molestie consequat, vel illum dolore eu feugiat nulla facilisis at vero eros et accumsan et iusto odio dignissim qui blandit praesent luptatum zzril delenit augue duis dolore te feugait nulla facilisi.

Lorem ipsum dolor sit amet, consectetuer adipiscing elit, sed diam nonummy nibh euismod tincidunt ut laoreet dolore magna aliquam erat volutpat. Ut wisi enim ad minim veniam, quis nostrud exerci tation ullamcorper suscipit lobortis nisl ut aliquip ex ea commodo consequat. Duis autem vel eum iriure dolor in hendrerit in vulputate velit esse molestie consequat, vel illum dolore eu feugiat nulla facilisis at vero eros et accumsan et iusto odio dignissim qui blandit praesentluptatum zzril delenit augue duis dolore te feugait nulla facilisi. Lorem ipsum dolor sit amet, consectetuer adipiscing eli, sed diam nonummy nibh euismod tincidunt ut laoreet dolore magna aliquam erat volutpat.

Ut wisi enim ad minim veniam, quis nostrud exerci tation ullamcorper suscipit lobortis nisl ut aliquip ex ea

Contents

1

Figure 5.2 Multiple Column Document

author can provide a document that has been 'tagged', so that it will convert into the house style of the publisher when imported into the page make-up system. Publishers can provide style-sheet information to the author to assist in this.

Laser printers may be used as typesetting devices for many book requirements. The artwork for this book, for example, was produced using a popular PC-based desktop publishing application and typeset on a laser printer.

For authors interested in self-publishing, the advent of desktop publishing has made the production of typeset artwork a much cheaper proposition.

TECHNICAL DOCUMENTATION PRODUCTION

The use of desktop publishing for the production of technical documentation is quite significant and remains on the increase. It is probably not surprising that desktop publishing is used by most computer industry related companies to produce manuals, instruction leaflets, technical specifications and other similar publications. The technology on which to run the page make-up software is often already available for such organisations.

Since most technical publications are printed in numbers of 250 copies or less (according to a Digitext survey), the use of laser printers for running out the actual production copies is fairly commonplace. For many organisations that need to produce technical manuals, some page make-up systems (notably Xerox Ventura and similar systems) are particularly suited to long document production of a style that varies little throughout the document, and can generate lists of contents, indexes, etc. For such users, desktop publishing offers the benefits of reduced cost per page, decreased production timescales with fewer proofing cycles (always important for documentation that has to accompany new product releases), and, especially, the ability to make frequent updates and changes to the basic publication.

Since graphics can be incorporated into the publication, technical documents can be illustrated and complete pages printed without the need for additional paste-up and artwork manipulation.

ADVERTISEMENTS

Text-based advertisements used in magazines and newspapers are ideally suited to production on a desktop publishing system. Job-vacancy adverts are a good illustration of this type of work. They are often enclosed in a box and use a variety of typefaces, with perhaps a logo, within the content, and usually little in the way of illustrations. Easily produced on a desktop publishing system, advertisement artwork is often produced in this way for local and national newspapers. The use of laser printers for producing the artwork is usually satisfactory for most newspaper publications. Although the resolution of laser printers falls behind phototypesetting, the low quality of paper on which newspapers are printed tends to negate this difference. Some local and national newspapers are now entirely typeset using laser printers instead of phototypesetters.

With laser printers that can handle A3 paper sizes, artwork and typesetting bureaux are now offering services for the production of the entire classified advertisements and property sales sections of local newspapers, using desktop publishing and laser printing.

Organisations that have their own desktop publishing systems can now typeset their own advertisements for publication, provided they have the measurements for the column widths of the publication available, though there are some publishing organisations who refuse artwork not produced by NGA union members.

VISUAL AIDS

Many organisations, especially those concerned with education and training, use visual aids for presentations, lectures and conferences. In particular, desktop publishing can be employed to produce overhead projector transparencies which are much clearer and more interesting than hand-written or typed versions. By using large, bold typefaces, transparencies can be made to convey their message with considerable clarity, which reduces the likelihood of complaints from those individuals towards the back of a lecture theatre who cannot normally read the projected typed transparencies which are often too faint.

Most laser printers will take special stationery for printing directly onto transparency film. This 'laser printer' or 'dry copier' film has a slightly rough surface on one side to permit the toner to adhere to the surface without smudging, and the film is thick enough to pass through the heated rollers without wrinkling or completely melting (beware of using ordinary transparency film for this reason, as it can ruin the laser printer).

Specialist hardware equipment is also available to produce 35mm colour transparencies. The software packages, which operate in a very similar style to desktop publishing, offer a variety of typefaces and graphics to make up presentation slides, which can be output to a device which projects the image, as seen on the screen, to a camera. Colour is provided by displaying the black and white image as a series of picture elements through coloured filters. The slide is exposed for about a minute or so as the various colours are overlaid. The software can then print a copy of the slides as a sheet of prompts with attached notes for use by the lecturer or presenter. Not strictly desktop publishing itself, however, this technology is an off-shoot from the process and development of desktop publishing.

PRINT AND DESIGN ARTWORK

Desktop publishing can be regarded as a tool for design just as much as a means to produce a specific output. In the hands of a graphic designer or typographer, the desktop publishing system can offer the opportunity to experiment with page elements, layout options and text styles for the purposes of producing roughs and proofs of publication and advertising work to clients. The ease with which graphic and text page elements can be manipulated makes the preparation of artwork easier than traditional cutting and pasting on the drawing board. By using real typeset text, the designer can get a better idea of what a finished page layout will look like without having to go to the expense of producing actual phototypeset artwork, or occupying the valuable time of the typesetter operator. Using the benefit of WYSIWYG screen displays, the designer can play around with ideas on the screen without having to use any paper and paste at all.

Some desktop publishing software systems may offer special effects not normally found on traditional phototypesetting devices, and these can offer the designer new ways to enhance the appearance of a layout; for example, shaded backgrounds of differing densities and the ability to rotate graphics and text elements a full 360 degrees.

Copy fitting and graphics manipulation facilities in desktop publishing help designers to arrange various layout elements to fit a particular amount of space. This is often important when planning a brochure or leaflet, or to ensure that a particular amount of column space in a newspaper or magazine is used effectively. Most page make-up systems permit graphic images, such as scanned photographs to be cropped and scaled to fit particular spaces, and with the ability to flow text around pictures and odd shapes, time spent at the design stage of any publication can be noticeably reduced.

Not all printers have their own in-house graphics and artwork facilities. Many small jobbing printers put out artwork and typesetting to specialists. This is because the cost of investment in phototypesetting equipment and skilled staff to operate it can be beyond the financial means of the company and the capital outlay may not be easily recovered in a short enough space of time without considerable expansion. With a complete phototypesetting installation costing upwards of £20,000, the attraction of desktop publishing is its relative cheapness to install. For as little as £3,000, a printer can acquire a computer and laser printer, with desktop publishing software which enables them to at least handle some of the artwork requirements, particularly for those jobs that do not warrant the ultimate quality of phototypesetting. Many of the High Street quick-print shops are now finding desktop publishing a useful aid to artwork production. You are just as likely to find wedding invitation cards printed on a desktop publishing system with a laser printer as any other means, and the time and cost savings help keep the prices down.

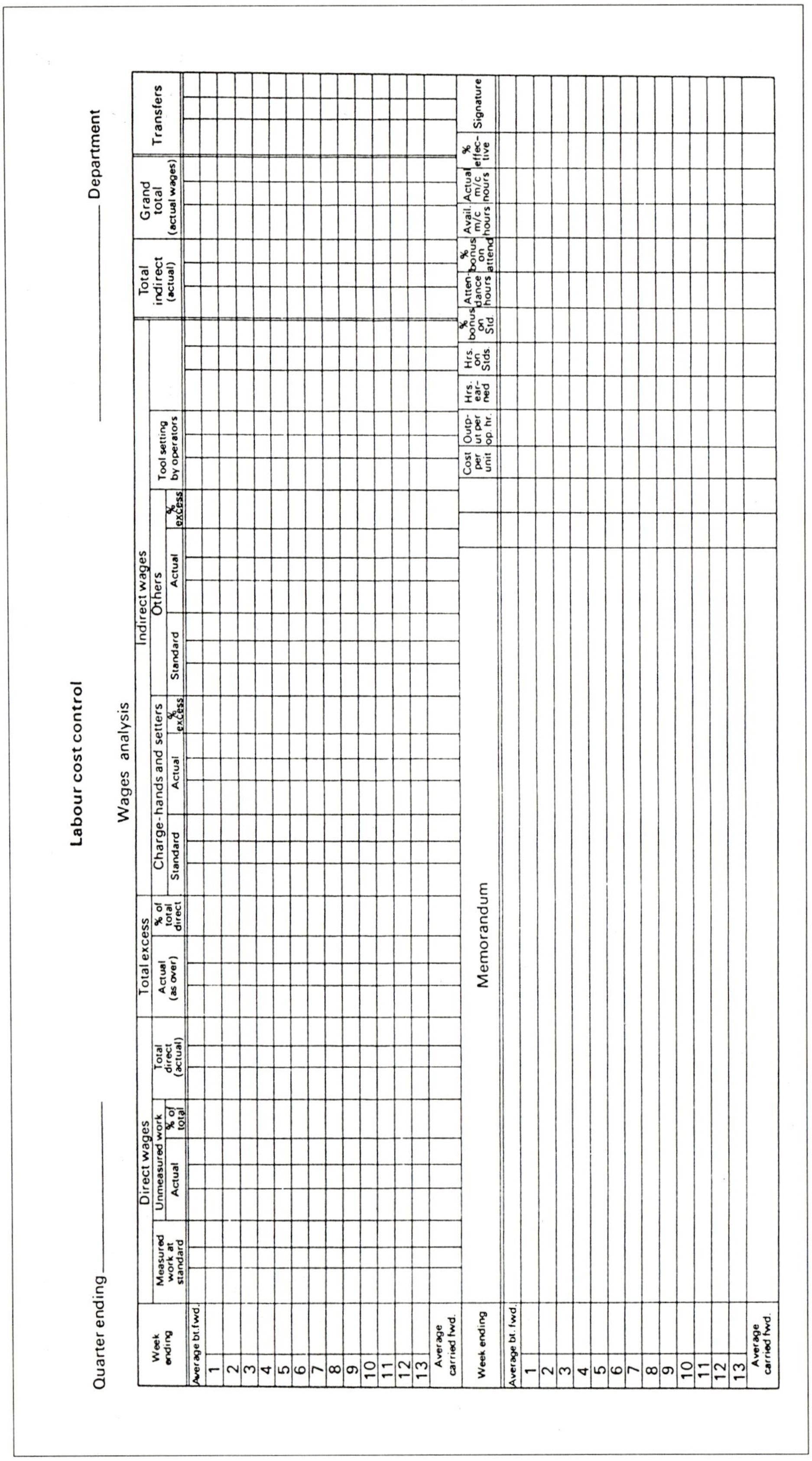
Labour cost control
Quarter ending ____________ Department ____________
Wages analysis
Week ending | Direct wages: Measured work at standard; Unmeasured work: Actual, % of total | Total direct (actual) | Total excess: Actual (as over), % of total direct | Indirect wages: Charge-hands and setters: Standard, Actual, % excess; Others: Standard, Actual, % excess; Tool setting by operators | Total indirect (actual) | Grand total (actual wages) | Transfers
Average bt. fwd.
1 2 3 4 5 6 7 8 9 10 11 12 13
Average carried fwd.
Week ending | Memorandum | Cost per unit | Outp-ut per op. hr. | Hrs. ear-ned | Hrs. on Stds | % bonus on Std. | Atten-dance hours | % bonus on attend | Avail. m/c hours | Actual m/c hours | % effec-tive | Signature
Average bt. fwd.
1 2 3 4 5 6 7 8 9 10 11 12 13
Average carried fwd.

Figure 5.3 Example Forms Work

FORMS WORK

Almost every organisation uses forms. Most of them are for internal use. They may include employment application forms, stores requisitions, parts lists, stocktake sheets, quality-control forms, time sheets, schedules, registers, score sheets, sales call sheets, analysis forms, exam marking cards and many more.

Desktop publishing software and a laser printer are an ideal way to produce these forms. For the small numbers needed, the laser printer can be used to print all the copies required. Alternatively a master copy can be produced which may then be photocopied in the required numbers. The great benefit of producing forms with desktop publishing is that boxes and rules, which all forms comprise, can be so easily drawn using a mouse pointing device. Furthermore, forms often require updating frequently. When the original layout is produced internally, changes can be made simply and swiftly at considerably lower costs than using the facilities of a printer or other external service. However, if multi-part sets are required, the desktop publishing system can only be used to produce the original artwork and printing and finishing will have to be handled elsewhere, but the benefit of controlling the content can at least reduce the artwork cost and save on proofs and time.

ACADEMIC AND EDUCATIONAL USE

Within the educational and training sphere, desktop publishing has its role to play, not only in the production of publications required by the organisation, but as a training aid in its own right. Students of art and design can learn much about the basics of design and typography using the facilities of a desktop publishing system, and for technology students, there is much that can be learned about the basic principles of printing technology.

Desktop publishing is fun to use; so many students will find the practical use of the system rewarding as well as informative. Printed results can be produced quickly which means that students can see the results of their efforts almost immediately and can learn about the various aspects of graphic effects and good layout from their experimentation with the system.

Of course, the system will be of benefit to the training or teaching establishment for the production of course material, presentation and visual aids. Like technical documentation, course notes are often subject to constant updating and revision, and the ability to be able to respond to this when printing new texts is an important consideration.

SUNDRY PRINTING JOBS

It is not uncommon for an organisation that has obtained a desktop publishing system to find many applications for printing and publish-

Figure 5.4 Sundry DTP Output

ing that were not previously considered. From invitations to menus, from notices to public signs, desktop publishing offers many additional possibilities for one-off print jobs, that would otherwise be ignored completely due to adverse cost, or produced with cheap and low-quality means.

The use of special stationery in the laser printer enables desktop publishing systems to print sheets of address labels, and since laser printers are quick and quiet compared to other printers, this can a very helpful resource for large mailings. Other similar sundry print jobs might include name badges (particularly useful for meetings and conferences or for security purposes), stock labels for goods and machinery parts, business cards, window stickers, posters, etc.

Given time, the number of possible applications within any organisation for desktop publishing will expand beyond those for which the system was originally intended. In fact, the ultimate use to which the system may be used could be completely different from the aims of the organisation when the system was first implemented.

6 Choosing a DTP System

Choosing a desktop publishing system means answering a lot of questions: questions about requirements, in terms of output quality and quantity, productivity, cost effectiveness, profitability and so on.

In order to establish the need for desktop publishing within an organisation, the manager must evaluate its publication requirements. What type of documentation is produced by the organisation for both internal and external use? In answer to this question, the manager will draw up a list of known publications – which might include some of the following:

Internal Forms (requisitions, etc)
Public Notices and Reports
Overhead Transparencies
Business Correspondence
Production Schedules
Badges and Name Tags
Company Magazines
Internal Reports
Meeting Minutes
Business Cards
Advertisements
Business Forms
Product Lists
Course Notes
Directories
Newsletters
Catalogues
Brochures
Mailshots

Accounts
Booklets
Journals
Notices
Labels
Signs

From the list of known publications, the manager then needs to identify the current methods employed for their production. This will almost certainly vary according to the type of publication and the quality required. Most internal documentation and business correspondence will probably be typed or word processed. The more complex publications, such as business forms, brochures, etc, will probably be produced using the services of external resources – printers, designers and advertising agents. The next stage is to ascertain what publications are desirable beyond those that are currently produced. For example, the marketing department might have proposed the idea of a newsletter to advertise the organisation's activities. As it is a new publication, there may be no obvious method of production based on existing publications.

In reviewing the publishing needs of the organisation, both existing and proposed, the manager may come to the conclusion that desktop publishing has a role to play in assisting with the production of any or all of the items listed. Choosing the right solution is then a matter of deciding what publication production is required and carrying out a feasibility study on the use of desktop publishing in meeting organisational objectives.

It may be that, as a result of the study, some of the publications not considered suitable for internal production could indeed be handled by the implementation of desktop publishing or graphics, thus reducing the burden on external resources, and reducing timescales and costs at the same time. Likewise, it may be found that, without considerable investment in both machine and human resources, the production of certain documents (especially high-quality publications) are beyond the scope of the organisation, and the use of electronic publishing systems would be an unnecessarily cumbersome and expensive route to take for what is adequately catered for using external services.

Decisions about choosing desktop publishing (and that includes choosing whether to use desktop publishing at all) must be made on the basis of several considerations surrounding the current methods of producing printed matter. To do this properly, a feasibility study should be undertaken, and some guidelines are given below.

THE FEASIBILITY STUDY

As a manager, you are probably aware of the need, when conducting a feasibility study, to appoint individuals to be responsible for the study, for gathering information and for managing and chairing the decision making process based on the results obtained from research. Someone will also need to be responsible for seeing that the study is carried out according to agreed timescales and that the appropriate information gathered is properly filtered and organised so that a conclusive management decision can be reached about the most suitable acquisition. In short, a steering committee must be organised. This may sound like a sledgehammer approach to cracking a nut, but there is no reason why the feasibility study should be complicated, too time consuming or unduly expensive. The entire feasibility study may be conducted by one person – if the situation warrants no more attention, in the opinion of the management. Indeed, you may appoint yourself as the sole investigator into the suitability of desktop publishing and the choosing of the most appropriate system. The basic principles of the study apply regardless of the size of the operation. A single decision by one person may substitute the debate of a steering committee, but the arguments considered and the process of decision making should not differ largely because of that.

The steering committee should be responsible for ensuring that all departments that may be affected by the acquisition of a desktop publishing system are involved, in whole or in part, in contributing towards the feasibility study. In the early stages, the following terms of reference should be on the agenda:

- to establish the use to which desktop publishing can be put;
- to gather information about the available technology;
- to investigate the present means by which publications are produced;
- to set a timescale for each stage of the study;
- to set an overall budget for the project;
- to identify who will be responsible for the system if one is obtained;
- to identify who will or can operate such a system.

All of the above points are heavily interwoven. It is clear that until some idea of the budget is established, it is not possible to know what type of desktop publishing system is affordable. Until this is done, you cannot assess the appropriate system for the intended purposes.

The aim of the feasibility study should be to establish whether or not the objectives set at the start of the project can be met under the terms of reference stated above and, if not, whether the terms of reference are to be modified, or whether desktop publishing is an unsuitable proposition.

EXISTING SYSTEMS

Having compiled a list of publications produced and distributed by the organisation it is worth drawing up a brief outline of the way each publication is currently prepared. Any existing cost information is worth gathering, particularly costs of external work carried out on specific publications. For example, if the organisation has produced a catalogue recently, and the accounts department have invoices for the work done on the job, it may be possible to establish direct costs for various elements of the production, such as typesetting, artwork, printing, etc. If the work is handled exclusively by an agent or printer, it may be difficult to establish the component costs of a print job. This will be the case if you have invoices or quotations that do not break down the cost elements of a publication.

For publications about which you have no cost information, you may try a pilot scheme of getting quotations for a dummy print job. You will need to be fairly accurate, however, about the nature of the job, such as use of colour, amount of text, number of photographs, type of paper used, etc, in order to get any sensible information from the exercise. For an organisation that has a department responsible for publications, this should be a matter for the manager in charge of that particular activity. Getting together information about current methods and costs helps focus on the suitability and effectiveness of current publication methods. Table 6.1 shows an example.

Name of Job: Product Price List			
Circulation	2,000		
Frequency of revision/reprint	Approx. every 3 months		
Originator of content	Sales Department		
Finish	A4 booklet - 4 sides		
Colour	One colour		
Illustrations	None		
Artwork by whom	Typographics Ltd	@	69.00
Printed by	Dalton Printers	@	975.00
Unit cost			0.63
Comments:	extra costs on proofs and artwork amendments worked out at about		216.00

Table 6.1 Print Job Analysis

Based on a collection of analysis information about the current print jobs, it is possible to identify those publications where desktop publishing can obviously make a contribution. For other jobs, the contributions may not be so clear. Considering the example in Table 6.1, it is probably the typesetting that could be produced on a desktop publishing system. The fact that it is done internally will mean that the proofing and amendment costs could probably be reduced also. However, the printing cost may not change (in this example, the printing cost includes plate making, imposition, printing, folding and stitching, plus the cost of paper). A quantity of 2,000 price lists of four sides each amounts to a total of 4,000 sheets of A4 paper (or 2,000 A3 folded) which is probably too high a quantity for a desktop laser printer to handle. Alternatively, one may have decided that the quantity could be handled by a laser printer because the usage of the 2,000 was over a reasonable period of time, and the fact that they are produced in-house means that they do not all have to be printed at once. Even so, if the job is printed in one colour, and that colour is a medium blue, a laser printer with a standard toner cartridge will not be able to reproduce in anything other than black, in which case one would need to decide whether to compromise and change colour for the sake of convenience.

This simple example illustrates some of the questions that need to be asked about every publication job on the list. To generalise these questions for every print job, you need to consider the following questions:

- Is the current method cost effective?
- Is the quality of the current method satisfactory (can it be improved or will you accept a lower quality)?
- Does the current method produce results quickly enough (can the timescale be reduced – does the timescale need to be reduced)?
- Would the use of desktop publishing improve any of the previous considerations?
- Would the use of desktop publishing cause any compromises in quality?

It should be remembered that at this stage in the process, the steering committee for the feasibility study is not looking for absolute answers to any of the above questions. Indeed, it may be fairly assumed that for the most part, the knowledge and information required to give specific answers is unlikely to be found from the members of the steering committee. The purpose of the exercise above is to guide the committee into a decision about the *likely* use of desktop publishing for applications, and the information gathered is there to assist in this exercise. Specific answers will come later when proposals are requested from potential sources of a desktop publishing system.

Assuming that the steering committee agrees that there is a place for desktop publishing on the basis of answers to some of the questions suggested previously, the next stage is to consider the selection process for a desktop publishing system. This is where decisions about budgets and organisational objectives come into play.

In deciding the objectives for selecting a desktop publishing system, the steering commitee must consider the overall organisational or departmental values; for example:

- Is there a cost saving to be made?
- Can the system be used to earn income?
- Is it technically practical to use a desktop publishing system?
- Are there people who can be trained to use it?
- Are there people who can be responsible for its ongoing use?
- Will a desktop publishing system integrate with existing systems?
- Will it provide indirect organisational benefits?

In considering the above points, the steering committee must evaluate both short-term and long-term benefits, in both subjective and quantifiable terms.

FINDING A SUPPLIER

Assuming that the steering committee agrees that desktop publishing has potential benefits for the organisation, the next stage is to establish a possible source of supply, and to encourage objective help from the suppliers in meeting the organisational needs. This can be done by short-listing two or three possible suppliers of desktop publishing systems. You will need to use more than one source since many computer and software suppliers who are vendors of desktop publishing are not necessarily any more experienced in its use and capabilities than you are. To protect against possible hard-selling techniques, the invitation of proposals from suppliers to satisfy your criteria will often help filter out the less suitable sources of supply.

Each supplier on the short list should be encouraged to propose possible system solutions to a list of requirements that are supplied by the steering committee.

In selecting a supplier, the following points should be considered:

- background and experience of the supplier in the field of desktop publishing;
- types of equipment sold (ie manufacturer) – this information will be needed to establish whether the systems supplied are likely to integrate with any existing hardware used within the organisation;
- maintenance and support facilities;
- pricing and other financial considerations;
- quality of personnel;
- training facilities provided;
- length of service;
- ability to supply reference sites.

SPECIFYING YOUR REQUIREMENTS

In order that a supplier may propose one or more solutions to your publishing needs, you must supply a specification of your requirements. This will be in the form of a document, or may be the result of a meeting or discussion with the supplier. Within the specification, you need to identify what the system is to provide, by when it is to provide it and what manner of publications you intend to produce. You must, at this stage, refrain from outlining your budget proposals, since the supplier is likely to present a solution that matches your budget, whether the solution is cheaper or not.

It is important to provide sufficient detail within your specification, so that the supplier's proposal remains as close to the organisation's intended requirements, but not so detailed as to prevent a creative approach to solving the problem. It is not uncommon for an organisation to have predefined their requirements too rigidly, and almost impose the solution on the supplier. The experience of the supplier may offer a solution that falls outside of the system requirements of the organisation, but which may have aspects that are of wider benefit to the organisation than may at first be apparent. For example, if the steering committee of the organisation believe that a certain type of desktop publishing will offer benefits for the production of certain, but not all, publications, they may fail to discover that a much more complex professional system, if installed, would have longer-term benefits, and solve production requirements for all publications.

The supplier making proposals must be allowed to offer advice on all issues of publishing within the organisation, so that any part of the feasibility study missed by the steering committee does not go by without due consideration.

To help understand the importance of this flexibility, the following example from a real-life situation illustrates how the resulting publishing solution varied considerably from the original intentions of the organisation involved.

The company in question produced a great deal of documentation to accompany its products. A separate publications department was responsible for this material, but did not play any part in the publication of other printed matter within the organisation. The marketing department handled the publication of brochures, price lists, leaflets, circulars and point-of-sale material. For these it used outside resources for artwork, typesetting and printing. The accounts department were responsible for the publication of the organisation's performance figures and the annual report and accounts. For this they used external resources, just like the marketing department. The administration department saw to the production of general printed matter such as forms, business stationery, business cards and all other sundry items. Only the publications department responsible for product handbooks and accompanying literature had any control over their own artwork production.

The organisation decided that, due to the amount of documentation that accompanied products (which constituted a reasonable proportion of the cost of sales), savings might be made by the implementation of desktop publishing for the production of artwork for the handbooks and manuals. Working on a budget of about £5,000, the manager of the publications department set about trying to find a practical solution to the requirement by investigating PC-based page make-up systems and a laser printer for artwork. After discussing the requirements with several suppliers and describing the nature of the publications that would need to be produced, one supplier asked about what other types of printed matter the organisation was producing. These were, of course, the publications of the marketing, accounts and administration departments, but since they were not part of the original brief, they were not considered important by the publications manager. However, as a result of investigating the possible cost justifications, a new proposal was taken to the organisation's management. This was by installing a complete digital phototypesetting system, and by employing a trained operator, there was a case for making considerable savings, in both time and expenditure, on the production of all of the artwork for the organisation's printed material – brochures, catalogues, the report and accounts, etc.

In this particular case study, the organisation found that the level of published material, largely due to the amount of product documentation involved, was sufficient to justify installing a professional system which would be employed 100% of the time.

Had the original intention of satisfying the system requirements of a PC-based desktop publishing system been adhered to, though there would have been quantifiable cost savings in the area of activity within the publications department, a lost opportunity would have resulted. For the organisation concerned, the publications department was expanded, and subsequently managed the publication of all printed matter for the entire company. All other departments funnelled work associated with printing through this one central source, and additional benefits, not previously quantifiable, in terms of improved timescales for production, better external resource control and consistent quality, were all realised.

SYSTEM DEMONSTRATIONS

Having short-listed suppliers, it is a good idea to arrange for demonstrations of possible system solutions. If you have particular publications that you think might be suitable for a desktop publishing application, offer these as examples, and invite the supplier to produce a sample of artwork based on them. This will enable you to ascertain whether the system is capable of producing the results and/or whether the supplier is sufficiently capable of operating the system, and therefore whether they are able to support it.

The demonstration may either be at the supplier's premises or at the client's site. If you are given a choice, it is better to have the demonstration at the supplier's premises, even if this means travelling some distance, for two reasons. Firstly, the supplier will have to hand (or should have) all relevant material, software and equipment that they supply. The course of a demonstration can often change as a result of the findings, and it may be that having begun a demonstration of one system, you end up seeing a completely different one. Secondly, you will be in an environment where there is less chance of interruption and distraction. If the organisation has appointed a steering committee for the feasibility study, it is best if one or two individuals are selected to attend demonstrations of the software and report back.

USING CONSULTANTS

If publishing forms a significant area of activity within the organisation, the selection of the right desktop publishing solution is more critical than for lesser requirements. This is especially so if it is deemed possible that an installation of more than one system is required to cope with the workload. Under these circumstances, the use of a consultant may be important in helping to make the right choice. The same may be true where an organisation has little or no previous experience of using computers for any other purpose. This complicates the selection procedure further, for choosing the right hardware and software together, for an organisation that might acquire computers for other purposes at a later stage, making the first move correctly can save considerable expense ahead.

The advantage of a computer consultant is that he or she will be able to advise on the current state of the desktop publishing market and suggest possible solutions in the light of the most recent technological developments. This is quite crucial in the computer industry since the technology advances so quickly. Even when you have acquired what you think to be the best solution in terms of a desktop publishing system, you will almost certainly find that one or more components of the system – for example, the laser printer is subsequently available as a much more comprehensive package, and at a much lower price. While you will never be insured against such advancements, which can often be frustrating after you have made a reasonable capital outlay, the use of consultants who know the market at least reduces the risk a little.

PRICE REDUCTIONS FOR EDUCATIONAL USE

If your organisation is an educational or training institution, ask suppliers about special price deals for the desktop publishing software and hardware. If you are looking to install several systems throughout your establishment, computer suppliers will often offer special discounts, handed down from the software and hardware manufacturers. The manufacturers have an interest in placing their products within training and educational establishments because it offers them an opportunity to show their products to people who could be potential customers when they leave the training environment. The choice of suitable desktop publishing systems could be influenced by this factor, especially if your budget is limited.

OTHER SOURCES OF INFORMATION

In carrying out the feasibility study for the selection of a suitable desktop publishing solution, the steering committee will need to gather as much information about current product offerings as is possible and practical within the timescales set in the initial terms of reference. Apart from supplier information, sales literature direct from manufacturers and demonstrations, the following means of gathering further details may be investigated.

Exhibitions

As an increasingly popular area of personal computing, desktop publishing affords quite a lot of attention at the many exhibition venues. At any general computer exhnibition, such as the Personal Computer Show or the Which Computer? Show, both held annually, you will find plenty of desktop publishing systems on show. You can get information, ask questions of the sales staff, see brief demonstrations, and make arrangements for obtaining further details of interesting systems, either by meetings or the sending on of literature and supplier addresses.

There are also exhibitions devoted to the topic of desktop publishing; for example, the International Desktop Publishing Show. At shows like this you will find desktop publishing hardware, software and peripheral equipment; and useful seminars and conferences often accompany such events and are an especially useful source of information to the newcomer. For details about when such events take place, you should either watch the computer press, or contact the major exhibition venues, such as the National Exhibition Centre, Wembley Exhibition Centre, Earls Court and Olympia, who can usually advise on forthcoming events.

Magazines

There are a wealth of weekly and monthly magazine publications devoted to computers and related topics. Among this material, you will often find articles and reviews which may help assist you in the selection process. You will also find many advertisements for desktop publishing related technology, and this is discussed again later in the chapter.

Books

There are many books on desktop publishing, all of which may provide further insight to the subject and give you a broader knowledge of what can be achieved using a desktop publishing system. Many books are available which are specific to particular page make-up software packages, and may be worth investigating if you have short-listed two or three possible packages, including those covered in the books. This is quite likely since packages for which books have been written are always going to be the most popular systems, such as Ventura and PageMaker, and, as such, are likely to be on any short list for consideration.

UNDERSTANDING ADVERTS AND SALES LITERATURE

It can be quite a difficult task for a novice to make sense of the advertisements and sales literature of any computer-related system. The industry is heavily infested with jargon words, and the advertisements make no concessions for a reader's lack of background knowledge.

Below are some guidelines to understanding the popular computer advertisements you are likely to see regarding desktop publishing. Together with the glossary, you may be able to comprehend a little more about what is being advertised.

Software

Software for desktop publishing use is often listed under the heading of DTP. In almost any list of software products in popular publications, you are likely to find the following two packages mentioned:

Xerox Ventura Publisher
Aldus PageMaker

These are the two forerunners of popular PC-based desktop publishing, with Ventura usually being a little more expensive than PageMaker. Both provide a number of similar features, though it is widely regarded that Ventura Publisher is best suited for long document production, like books and manuals, whereas complex and varied page layouts are not easy to handle, though Ventura can be used to produce them. In the field of page make-up and the more complex layout, PageMaker is the more popular choice. With recent developments in the software, enabling it to cope with documents of up to 128 pages in length, it is considerable competition for Ventura. PageMaker is available on both IBM PC-compatible equipment and the Apple Macintosh, but Ventura is not available for the Apple machine.

Prices will vary from one advert to another, and sometimes by a considerable amount. Be wary of foreign imports. These are often sold for considerably less than the normal price for the package in this country. For example, USA versions of Ventura sell cheaply in the UK but may not offer all the same features (for example, no standard A5 page layout, which is replaced by American Octavo size paper which is slightly narrower and longer than A5). You will also need to consider the support aspect of a foreign software package. If in doubt, ask the supplier whether the software is a genuine UK version if you are using it in the UK, or a USA version if using it in the USA. Some advertisements will qualify this anyway.

You are unlikely to find the more professional electronic publishing systems listed in popular advertisements. These systems are extremely comprehensive and may be the most suitable for your requirements, so do not forget that, however many advertisements you see, PageMaker and Ventura are by no means the only solutions.

Other software listed is likely to be packages that emulate one or other of the above. For example Timeworks is a popular alternative system to Ventura Publisher, operating in much the same way and with almost identical functions.

In association with the actual desktop publishing software itself, you may see something like the following:

'including GEM Desktop'
'Windows compatible'
'needs Microsoft Windows'

Both Gem and Windows are trade names for operating systems. These are items of software that control the operating of other software programs. Earlier in the book, the WYSIWYG style of screen display, with pull-down menus and mouse control, was explained. These interfaces between the operator and the computer were copied from the style adopted by the Apple Macintosh computer during the early 1980s. For other microcomputers, such as the IBM PC and compatibles, a different operating system is required to emulate this style of interface. The operating systems that allow this are actually software packages in their own right. Often they are supplied as part of the package accompanying a microcomputer; otherwise they can be bought separately. The operating systems of Gem and Microsoft Windows provide desktop publishing systems with this special kind of interface facility.

Other software items listed under the heading of DTP are likely to be accessories, and not actually page make-up systems themselves. Two of these that seem to crop up quite regularly are:

GoScript
Typographica

GoScript is actually a software utility that enables a desktop publishing package to send a PostScript formatted document to a non-PostScript laser printer. The software is currently available in two versions, offering a number of fonts that are 'scaleable' (ie you can have typefaces in a wide variety of sizes incremented by small units).

Typographica is a soft font supplier that sells typefaces which can be downloaded to a laser printer, to extend those already provided by the laser printer itself. For non-PostScript laser printers, which may often have a limited range of fonts available as a built-in capability, soft fonts offer an alternative way of extending the fonts available to a desktop publishing system. They are installed separately from the page make-up software, and are accessed whenever a document is to be printed using the fonts that have been installed. Typographica fonts are sold in both packages of several typefaces, or a single typeface family.

Hardware

Under the DTP heading in adverts, one is likely to find the most common hardware mentioned is laser printers. Since the computers on which many desktop publishing systems operate are standard personal computers, they are rarely listed unless the supplier is offering a complete desktop publishing package, including computer, printer and software.

Laser printers listed in adverts are numerous, but many are in fact 'badged' versions of the same printer. You basically have a choice of two types of laser printer – PostScript and non-PostScript. In an advert listing laser printers like the ones illustrated below:

Epson	6ppm	£1,595
Qume Crystal II	6ppm	£1,495

HP LaserJet II	8ppm	£1,999
Qume Publisher	6ppm	£2,999
Canon LBP-811	8ppm	£1,995
QMS PS-810+	8ppm	£4,500

the odd ones out, as far as price go, are the Qume Publisher and the QMS PS-810+. Both of these are, in fact, PostScript printers; the others are PCL printers (see Chapter 4 for an explanation of the difference). It is typically the case that laser printers which seem to be about £1,000+ more expensive than the others are often PostScript printers. Other factors that affect price are the speed of the printers (6ppm means that the maximum output speed is 6 pages per minute, 8ppm means 8 pages per minute) and the number of paper trays provided. You can have laser printers that have more than one paper tray, just like a photocopier, and some will print double sided in one operation. These can appear to be as expensive as PostScript laser printers, but are in fact PCL printers – so check before you get excited about the price.

The resolution of laser printers is rarely listed. In most cases you can take it to be 300 dpi unless otherwise stated.

A popular PostScript printer often listed is the Apple Laserwriter. Because this laser printer uses the PostScript language, it is suitable for connection to a microcomputer that outputs PostScript formatted documents and graphics. Therefore, do not think that it is only suitable as a peripheral device for use with Apple microcomputers such as the Macintosh. It is equally suitable for use with IBM compatibles.

Scanners are other hardware devices often listed. These tend to be priced at around £1,000 or more, but there are a few which cost as little as £200. These are hand-held scanners and are useful low-cost accessories, but have limited convenience if the original document to be scanned is large or good high-resolution quality is required. Scanners may be listed as having a resolution of perhaps 400 dpi. The higher the resolution of the scanner the more detailed is the image it can process. However, if your laser printer is 300 dpi resolution, then no matter how high the resolution of the scanner, you cannot print out at any higher resolution than that of your printer. The word 'flatbed', seen in association with scanners is simply a term for scanners that lie flat on the desktop with a horizontal surface on which the original is placed, rather like a manually operated photocopier. The alternative method of operation is a revolving drum, where the original does not lie flat (more like a facsimile machine).

Accessories

Accessories listed among the DTP adverts often include memory upgrades for laser printers. Most PostScript laser printers have sufficient memory built-in to cope with complex graphics and multiple typefaces. PCL printers, however, do not often come supplied with as much memory. If they are to cope with such things as downloadable typefaces and graphics, they often need to have additional memory slotted in. Memory upgrades are supplied in various packages; the more expensive they are, the more memory supplied.

Mouse attachments for microcomputers are also often advertised and prices range from £100 or less. Mouse packages often include 'free' software such as a drawing or painting facility.

Interfaces with Word Processing and Graphics

Most product specifications and brochures associated with desktop publishing software list the word processor and graphics software application with which they will interface; in other words, which types of document or picture format the desktop publishing system can 'read'. It is worth checking these lists to see, for example, if a word processor that your organisation may already use is listed among them. If so, you will find it much easier to transfer documents from the word processor to the page make-up facility. If it is not listed, there may be another way of transferring documents, particularly if your word processor offers more than one way of storing a document on disk. To be on the safe side, check with your word processor supplier as well. The same applies to graphics packages, though many of these use specific terms to identify picture file formats, and you simply need to see if they match with your own system's output.

THE NEXT STAGE

Assuming that a conclusion is reached about the desktop publishing system to be used, the next series of considerations will be about the implementation of the system, and that includes installation, training and on-going support. These points are covered in the following chapter.

7 Implementation

Having chosen your desktop publishing solution, the acquisition of the system depends upon the components that you need. If you already have computers available for use and even a laser printer or other output device in operation, the desktop publishing system will be in the form of a software package only. The purchasing decision in this case is usually a simple cash transaction.

If hardware (computers, laser printers, scanners, phototypesetters, etc) is also part of the acquisition the magnitude of the purchase is much more significant, and may be achieved by one of three means:

a) the equipment may be purchased outright, together with a suitable maintenance contract for technical and mechanical support, bought on a year-by-year basis;

b) the equipment may be rented or hired from a company, where the maintenance is often included in the hire agreement and as part of the hire charge;

c) the equipment may be leased (or lease-purchased), using a leasing company, where the cost is spread over a number of years.

Whichever way you choose to obtain the equipment, the technology you buy will be 'out-of-date' very quickly. This does not mean that it will be useless. So long as the equipment continues to do the job for which it is intended, it hardly matters whether the technology is old, so long as you can continue to obtain support and maintenance. In the computer industry, technology is 'old' after about two years, and out-of-date within one year.

The implementation of a chosen desktop publishing system can be broken down into the following actions:

- planning the use (distribution and personnel);
- installation;
- training;
- resource management.

Each of these is discussed in the paragraphs that follow.

PLANNING THE USE

This stage of the implementation involves decisions about the distribution of the facility within the organisation. It may be that the organisation's needs are simple and straightforward, and that a clear-cut decision about the use of the system can be made. Where the technology may affect more than one area of activity, the decisions required are a little more involved. For organisations that handle a variety of publications, from sales literature through to company printed matter (such as forms and reports, to newsletters and documentation) the availability of the resource to various departments may need some planning.

A wide distribution of the resource may be planned in cases where members of different departments need access to the page make-up facilities simultaneously. This may involve the use of computer networks, sharing resources such as laser printers and scanners. If the workload only justifies the employment of one computer, this may need to be centrally located to facilitate the accessibility for the various departments. The marketing department, for example, may need access to the facility to enable mailing and newsletter artwork to be produced. Other departments may wish to have access to the facility for the production of reports or visual aid material. The sales department may need facilities for product specifications, prices lists and so on. If the organisation already has an in-plant printing or publishing department, this is usually the obvious choice for siting the desktop publishing system, since the department is already a recognised source of design and artwork facilities. Where no such department exists, the location of the resource may depend on where it is most likely to be used, or it may need to be centrally located with equal access from all departments (see Figure 7.1). The marketing department of a company possibly being the second choice after the publications department.

Choosing the siting of the facility brings into question the personnel who will use it on a day-to-day basis and those who will have access to it on an ad-hoc basis. Decisions about the personnel to use it must

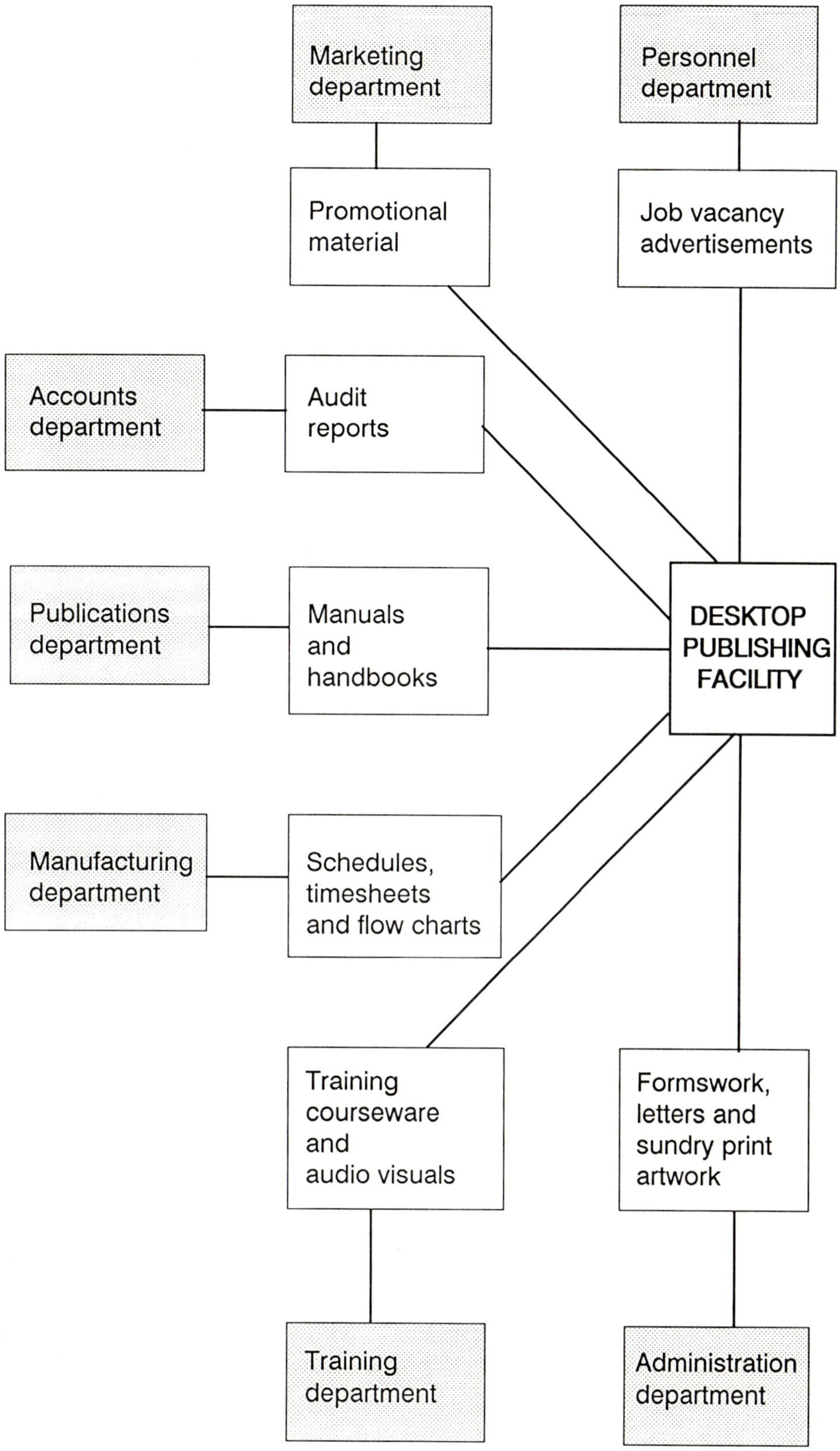

Figure 7.1 Accessibility to DTP Within the Organisation

depend upon who are suitable as operators, who will supervise and manage the resource and to what degree control over the security and priority of access to the system needs to be taken. These points are discussed later in the chapter.

You will need to identify the personnel who will initially use the system, and the most suitable location before you actually carry out the installation. If a system is installed by a supplier, and training is to accompany the installation, decisions on these matters must have been taken beforehand.

INSTALLATION

Installation of the system may be tackled from one of two directions. Either the supplier carries out the installation for you, or your organisation takes on the task itself, having purchased the components of the system. If you choose to install the system yourself, because you feel you have sufficient experience of computer systems within your organisation, it is a good idea to ensure that you have recourse to a source of technical support in case of difficulty. This may be provided by a telephone hotline service from the supplier or manufacturer. In case of difficulties, you can then contact an expert for advice.

Most organisations will carry out their own installation of desktop publishing if they simply source a supply of software and hardware, purchased by mail order or from a High Street retailer, for the sake of saving on costs. If you follow this route, you are advised to seek some independent training for the system as soon as practical. This is not very expensive, and will certainly repay itself in the long term (see section on training below).

If you leave the installation to the supplier, you will expect that there will be some initial operator training on how to load and run the desktop publishing software. If you are using specialised peripheral equipment, such as laser printers or scanners, you will need basic instructions on how to operate the equipment. For example, with a laser printer, you should find out how to feed paper into the printer, how to change toner cartridges, how to deal with paper jams, how to load and select fonts, how to connect the printer to the computer and configure the computer to recognise the printer, and regular simple maintenance, such as cleaning of rollers and guide wires, etc.

A successful installation can make the difference between a smooth running operation in the long run, or the short-term disaster that poor computer installations often cause. Unfortunately, one often has to rely on the hope that a supplier will have the experience and knowledge to ensure a smooth installation first time around. If you know of any other establishments which have also installed and are successfully using desktop publishing, they may be a useful source of advice about potential pitfalls, which only experience can uncover.

A visit to an establishment using desktop publishing for similar applications to your own organisation's requirements can be a particularly educational experience, and your supplier may be able to assist you in finding a reference site for this purpose, based on other clients they have serviced. You will probably only be afforded the luxury of such a visit having made the acquisition of your system, or at least raised the appropriate purchase agreements with the supplier, who may not otherwise be keen to disturb other clients on your behalf, unless there are serious business opportunities in the offing.

TRAINING

To obtain the best results from the desktop publishing system, the persons operating the system should be adequately trained. It is not sufficient to consider that a word processor operator will make an easy or natural transition to desktop publishing, and any report or sales hype that suggests that this is the case should be ignored. There is an advantage for a word processor operator in so far as they have learned keyboard skills and may be familiar with the operation of computers and disk housekeeping, but the specific skills of page make-up have to be taught to the operator properly. Many of the software packages include guidance on layout and design, and some provide templates (sample layouts which can be used as the basis for documents of a certain type), but these are only superficial aids.

The most immediate source of training must come from the supplier of the system. It is likely to concentrate on the operation of the system's features, how to select functions and perform basic operations such as page set-up, editing and printing. The training is almost certainly going to exclude the broader concerns of good design, or how to make the most of the facilities provided. For this, you may have to seek the services of independent training organisations.

Training in the area of good design is essential if the desktop publishing system's facilities are not to be abused. As one training organisation's literature put it:

> 'Desktop publishing is here! Now, by using a personal computer and laser printer to prepare documents for print, your organisation can dispense with the services of professional typesetters and graphic artists. Yes, you too can churn out messy, boring, confusing documents more productively than you ever believed possible...!'

This message sums up the importance of training. Indeed, it may be regarded as a warning for those who ignore the need to provide adequate training for the staff involved in using the system.

A company called Popular Communication Courses Ltd, at Bridgnorth, who run training courses on the subject of desktop publishing emphasise the need to look beyond simply the acquisition of suitable software and hardware. They suggest that an individual within the organisation should be given the job of supervising the introduction of desktop publishing – someone prepared to be the in-house DTP expert, who will consider how the implementation of desktop publishing will fit in with existing in-plant services or outside printers, and with existing arrangements for those responsible for gathering, writing and editing information.

Some training courses offer a mixture of advice on how to use desktop publishing with guidance on the selection of various systems. If you have already made a decision on the choice of desktop publishing system, beware of courses that seem to be for users of desktop publishing, but which in fact concentrate on matters that relate to the choosing and selecting of a suitable system.

The typical type of content that should be looked for in a training course for the operators of desktop publishing might include some of the following items:

- Overview of page make-up
- Basics on how a laser printer works
- Fundamentals of typography
    - Fonts, typefaces and styles, font families
    - Measurement systems – pica, points and ciceros
    - Type design – serifs and san serifs
    - Justification of text
    - Spacing and leading (including kerning)
- Layout principles and design elements
- Choosing the right layout for the job
- Proper use of white space
- Use of rules, boxes and other graphics
- Photographs – scanning and screening
- Special typographic effects
- Hyphenation
- Understanding the WYSIWYG interface (using the mouse)
- Soft fonts
- Using templates and style sheets
- Understanding graphics file formats
- Printing out
- Basics of print processes
- Phototypesetting with DTP
- Using generic coding and interfacing with bureaux

Within the course structure, the subjects of design and layout should cover a number of typical publication types, eg newsletters, magazines, reports, brochures, technical documentation, etc.

If you have a number of staff who will be involved in desktop publishing within the organisation, then, provided numbers are high enough, it may be financially viable to hire the services of a tutor in the subject, who can gear a course specifically towards your organisation's particular requirements. However, you must ensure that adequate facilities are provided for this, since one of the benefits of off-site training is that the right environment for learning is provided – away from the phones and other distractions of the working establishment. In deciding who should be trained in the basics of desktop publishing, you should consider the following individuals:

- operators of DTP (or those who *will* be operating it);
- supervisors and the manager of the system;
- marketing staff who need to appreciate the possibilities of the improved communication facilities;
- graphics and design staff employed in an in-plant publications department;
- technical authors.

RESOURCE MANAGEMENT

This aspect of the implementation procedures ensures that the newly acquired facilities are installed and distributed according to the intentions of the steering committee, previously responsible for the stages up to and including acquisition. The continued use of the resource must be properly managed, and the following chapter deals with the maintenance of standards and review of the technology within the organisation. In the initial stages, however, the responsibility for resource management includes putting into place the mechanism which determines how desktop publishing is to be used within the organisation, on what sort of jobs, and how priorities are assigned to possible work schedules.

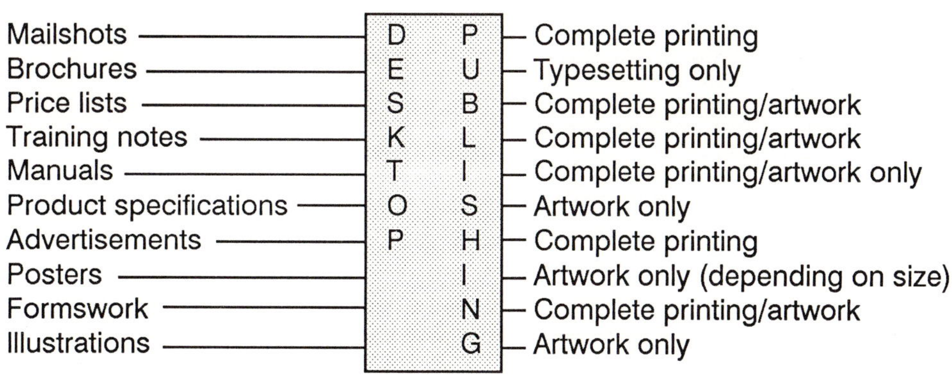

Figure 7.2 Contribution of DTP to Publications

Desktop publishing often provides a mixed contribution towards various publications. In some cases, desktop publishing may provide a total solution to the preparation, production and printing of a document. In other cases, it may contribute towards producing artwork which will then be processed further using outside resources (see Figure 7.2).

The individuals responsible for resource management of desktop publishing must evaluate the most appropriate applications for the system. This involves further analysis of the methods currently employed to produce the currently produced printed matter. Some of the information in this respect may have already been gathered by the steering committee during the feasibility study. Once the system has been installed, this information must be re-evaluated and revised.

On the results of an independent survey, the following applications of desktop publishing were among the information gathered:

Application	% of use for DTP
Advertisements	16
Directories	5
Forms	32
Installation Manuals	35
Marketing Brochures	35
Newsletters	43
Price Lists	29
Product Data Sheets	40
Reports	35
Reference Manuals	48
Sundries (correspondence)	46

From this it can be seen that desktop publishing applications are quite varied. They are particularly popular for the production of manuals and similar instruction and reference documentation and for newsletters. Other desktop publishing applications mentioned in the survey, but with less than 3% of usage included proposals, journals, books, notes, flyers, course notes and audio/visual aids.

In the same survey, an attempt was made to establish whether the desktop publishing system was used to produce only artwork (for use in printing by conventional means), or was used to produce the printed, finished documents too. The results showed that conventional print methods were still favoured, with the majority of desktop publishing output of the above listed applications being for artwork only, especially where the print runs were high.

If the desktop publishing system is properly supervised, the supervisor will be responsible for assigning priorities to the various tasks that will be carried out, after consultation with the departments for whom the work is intended. If no supervisor is appointed, a manager should ensure that the operator is given guidelines about sensible priorities for handling work that may be brought directly to them. For example, one could set up an 'in tray' system for work to be processed on the page make-up system, but there needs to be a proper system for prioritising jobs other than on a first-come, first-served basis. If a system of prioritising work is properly set up, the information about this system should be circulated to those departments concerned.

In addition to managing the type of applications for desktop publishing, a proper system should be set up to ensure that sufficient material resources are available. This includes the sourcing and supply of paper, toner, phototypesetting materials, overhead transparencies and other consumable items associated with desktop publishing. If the operator(s) of the system is to be responsible for the control of materials usage, ensure that they have adequate access to purchasing facilities for these items.

Within large organisations, and especially educational establishments, where there may be many people who need access to the desktop publishing system, it may be necessary to ensure proper security. This means making sure that unauthorised access to the facility is prevented, so that damage to systems and valuable data does not inadvertently result from misuse of the facility. There are many ways of controlling access, though this will largely depend upon the administration within the organisation. Possible ways of controlling access are to have a supervisor in charge of the system, using a security device on the computer, such as password control or key lock control, or by simply restricting the availability of the resource to only those individuals who have a genuine need for it. You must ensure that the desktop publishing system is not misused by individuals typesetting themselves party invitations, posters and other personal documents, unless you deliberately make the system available for private use of the individual operators.

As a final responsibility of resource management, it is necessary to ensure the proper integration of the desktop publishing system with existing systems. These include current methods of producing printed matter, and computer systems currently used for word processing, graphics origination and similar functions. The transfer of data files from word processors and graphics software packages to a page make-up system needs to be properly organised. A procedure for the storing, updating and filing of text and pictures should be implemented so that there is not a situation where different formats of various documents are used, when this may be unnecessary.

You need to begin as you mean to go on. For example, if documents are originated on word processors, you should establish how these are to be updated after editing. Once transferred to the desktop publishing system for page make-up, you should decide whether corrections to the document subsequently made on the publication files of the desktop publishing system are also mirrored in the original word processed documents (assuming they are to be kept at all). Alternatively, you may choose to import text to the page make-up system, and make all future additions using the desktop publishing system alone, then exporting the file again into word processor format only if the document needs to be used as the basis of another original.

The theme of resource management is continued in the following chapter, in respect of ongoing review and control of the use of desktop publishing within the organisation.

8 Standards and Review

The management of the desktop publishing resource should be an ongoing process. By measuring standards, and reviewing the suitability and performance of the system, the organisation can be assured of obtaining the maximum benefit from the system. This is concerned with identifying what it is you need to review so that you know whether a desktop publishing system is being of maximum benefit. Whether a system is precisely achieving its goals depends on what you decide your goals are. For example, if you install desktop publishing with a view to simply having more control over your own print jobs, then this may be an easy goal to achieve, which is simply measured in terms of how much more artwork your organisation produces on the desktop publishing system compared to the situation prior to installation. For most installations, however, the acquisition of a desktop publishing system embraces a much wider set of goals.

The success of desktop publishing within an organisation is measured in two distinct areas: the ability of the system to achieve practical results, such as reducing artwork costs, timescales, providing more direct control over the content of printed documents, etc, and the ability of the system to improve or at least maintain standards and the quality of publication designs. The first are quantifiable results of implementing desktop publishing, whereas the other aspects are more subjective, and probably need some clarification.

WHAT CONSTITUTES GOOD QUALITY OUTPUT?

Many articles concerned with desktop publishing discuss the fact that the purchase of a typesetting system may provide the tools to produce high-quality printed output, but does not give the skills. Much criticism has been thrown at the new technology from printers and other professionals of the design trade who maintain that the widespread use of desktop publishing has been responsible for a growing trend of poor quality publications, and go as far as describing the output as messy, illegible garbage. If your organisation is in the print, advertising or design business, you will already understand the importance of good layout. If your organisation is not associated with these trades, you may be wondering whether these professionals are merely protecting their interests, or whether they have a genuine reason for being critical of the output from most desktop publishing users. To put the question another way – is there such a thing as a good page layout, or is it a totally subjective matter?

Trying to answer this question is rather like trying to explain what makes a good painting. In many people's eyes, a Picasso or a Van Gogh might be an appalling example of painting, and they would never have such images hanging on their walls. Such a judgement is a matter of taste, and we are all entitled to our opinions in such cases. There is no doubt, however, that the same paintings are also regarded as some of the finest examples of art. Can the same apply to a page design?

Well, there is one aspect that may be shared in this analogy, and it may not be immediately obvious. Both the painting examples and printed documents are *communicating*. A painting might be trying to communicate a feeling, impression, idea, emotion or some other abstract entity, and a printed document is trying to communicate something to its reader. The difference is that a printed document is perhaps more obvious in what it is trying to communicate, but whether it achieves this is as much a matter for the design as it is for the content. It is true that the words contained within a publication must communicate the message to the reader. Design helps or hinders by the way in which it both attracts and maintains the attention of the reader. A cumbersome page that looks like 'heavy reading', with little white space and dense areas of text, might dissuade someone from reading it, especially if they have little time. In the commercial environment, there is a considerable amount of printed matter that passes from department to department, and between various organisations. The content of much of this material either conveys essential business information (especially if the documentation is internal), or else it is intended to sell goods and services. In both cases, the communication of the content of the document is often important.

The first thing the publication must do is grab the attention of the reader. It must be appealing, or at least not consciously off-putting. Next, the design must help the reader take in the information by offering an ordered, logical structure, which guides the eye to the most important features. Having achieved these fundamental objectives, the design of the document can then afford to include purely aesthetic characteristics for the benefit of adding style and identity.

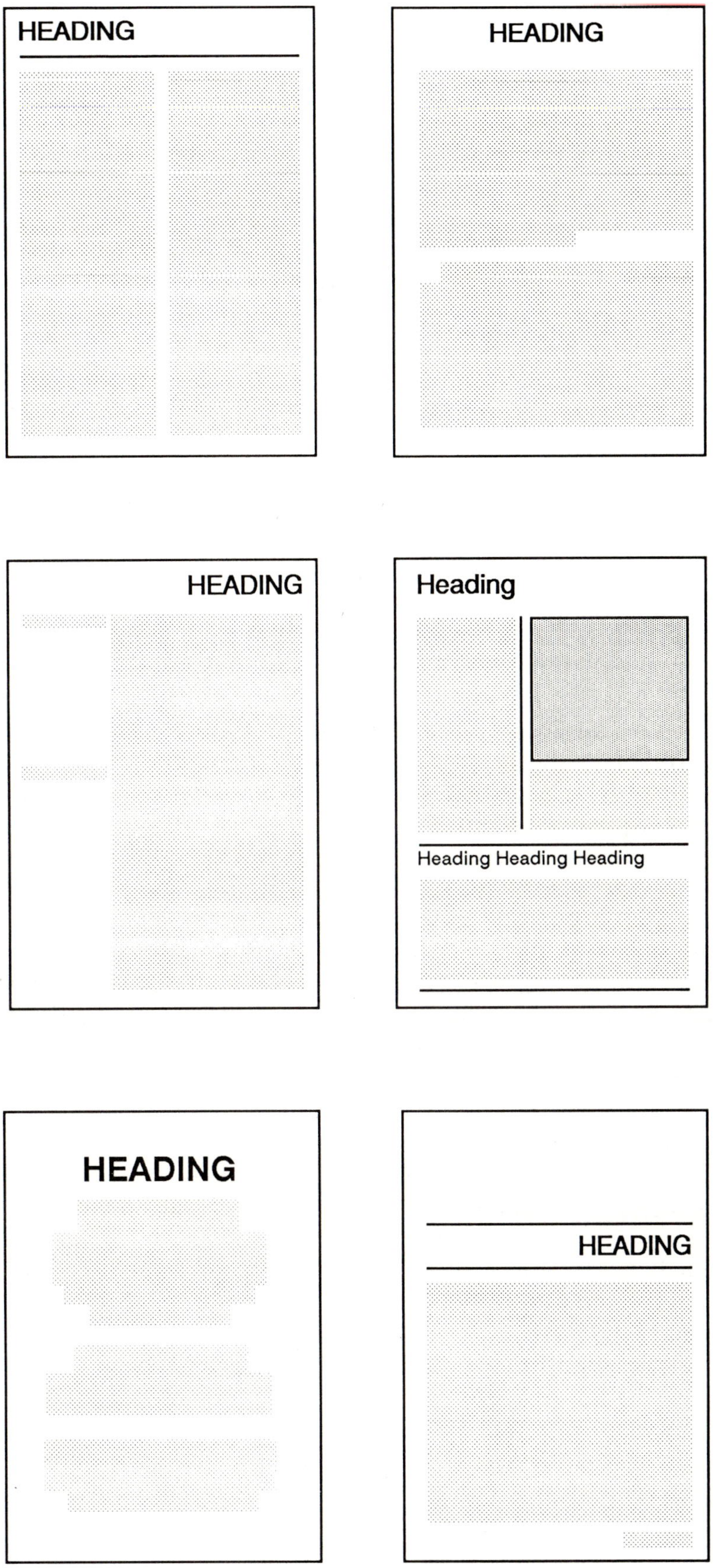

Figure 8.1 Design Comparisons

Typography is the art of designing printed matter. Desktop publishing systems provide facilities to assist in the typographical construction of a document, as opposed to a word processor which is merely concerned with the content. The more degree of control one has over the design elements, how they are arranged, how space is used to good effect, how the style of the type is used to highlight words, pinpoint headings and create interest in appearance, are all functions of the typographical controls of a document. This is why the 'professional' desktop publishing systems, as they are generally referred to, such as those previously categorised in this book as electronic publishing systems, have many more typographical controls than the more straightforward and cheaper systems. In addition, the degree of control offered by the typographical aspects of the system may be much finer.

The purpose of re-emphasising these design aspects is that, when reviewing the quality of output, or when establishing standards for the use of desktop publishing within your organisation, you are ensuring that the finished product of desktop publishing is doing its job properly – communicating the content effectively, and upholding the quality image of your organisation at the same time.

If you install desktop publishing software and a laser printer in the hope of achieving the same quality results as a team of professional designers, using phototypeset output, you will almost certainly fail to maintain quality standards. There are cases where this can happen, although unintentionally, because an organisation that has acquired a facility for typesetting feels that, in the interests of reducing overheads and expenditure, the desktop publishing system should be employed in the use of all typesetting requirements of the company, without considering whether the system's output is compromising the quality of the publication, compared to using outside resources. In order to avoid such pitfalls, one needs to implement procedures to regularly review the success of desktop publishing within the organisation, and the following paragraphs offer suggestions in this direction.

CONTINUING TRAINING

The maintenance of trained staff is important with any computer applications, and desktop publishing systems are no exception. If operators and other staff experienced in the use of desktop publishing leave the organisation's employment, it is very important to ensure that replacements are properly trained. It is often the case that replacement personnel receive far less formal training, compared to operators when a new system is first implemented, and it is often left to the leaving employee to hand over responsibilities to the newcomer. In the event of staff changes, training should be available for all aspects of desktop publishing.

A further point on this subject is the re-training of individuals, where new technology has been introduced and existing desktop publishing systems have been upgraded to keep up with the latest developments.

Once a new system is taken on board, those who are initially responsible for its immediate use are most likely to receive the initial training given at the time of installation. It is worth remembering that other individuals, who may come to use the technology at a later date, may also need this background knowledge, and there will be times when, in the absence of the originally trained operators (perhaps due to holidays or illness) other staff members may need to take temporary responsibility for the smooth operation of the system. To plan for such circumstances by offering fundamental training, is by far the best way to insure against loss in productivity at the most critical times.

STANDARDS AND QUALITY CONTROL

This area is probably one of the most difficult areas of review for an organisation unless it employs personnel skilled in the profession of print design or typography. For those organisations who do have such persons, they should be given the responsibility for ensuring that the standards and quality of the output from the desktop publishing system, which may be operated by many other individuals, is sufficiently high.

Unfortunately, it is the lack of training in the field of typography that is responsible for the way in which many organisations using desktop publishing produce poor designs in complete ignorance.

In order to achieve good quality in circumstances where the staff operating the system are relatively inexperienced, there are two possible ways to deal with the problem. One is to select an individual of suitable aptitude for attending one or more courses and seminars on desktop publishing design. There are a number of organisations who specialise in this field. The individual concerned becomes responsible for implementing guidelines and assistance to all operators of the system, in the areas of design and layout. It is a good idea to draw up a set of standards and housestyles which represent a ‘corporate’ identity. This is rather like having a set of rules governing the choice of typefaces for particular jobs, how the organisation’s name, address and logo are to appear on documents, what layout guidelines to follow for particular print jobs, and so on. The operator follows the housestyle rules according to the type of publication work being processed, and a certain amount of consistency can be achieved throughout the organisation and throughout the various documents published by it.

The second way of introducing quality control in an organisation where the operators have limited experience, is to call upon the services of independent specialists. There are now a number of services advertising help, support and consultancy in the field of desktop publishing. This can vary, from a telephone support facility to a design service in which the document layouts, the templates and style sheets used as the basis for a publication, are designed for you by professionals. Your operators then use the templates on the desktop publishing system according to the type of work being processed, and consistency of standards is maintained.

Such organisations have emerged as a result of recognising the considerable lack of knowledge and experience that users of desktop publishing systems have in the field of design. The situation is, perhaps, unique in the field of computing, where this new technology, which is essentially a specialist tool for professionals, has found itself in widespread use, and is one of the most popular and best-selling areas of personal computing in recent years. Above all, the quality control of the implementation of desktop publishing should be given a high priority, so that the transition to electronic publishing methods can be made without a compromise in the quality of the organisation's printed matter.

CYCLIC REVIEW

Cyclic review is simply the term for regular monitoring of the performance and application of a system, based on a predetermined checklist of questions and considerations (rather like a checklist of points to investigate when a car is serviced at regular intervals). Cyclic review systems help ensure that the objectives that were originally set for the application of desktop publishing remain satisfied, and to highlight any points that require attention or change. A hypothetical checklist is given below:

- Does the system meet the requirements of the organisation?
- Are the operational staff satisfied with the system?
- Are the management satisfied with the results?
- Does the system continue to integrate with other computer systems?
- Are there sufficient trained staff to operate the system at all times it is required?
- Is the output quality high enough?
- Are the intended applications still satisfied?
- Has the system expanded its application since the last review?
- Has the system reduced the cost of publications as intended?
- Has the system reduced the turnaround time for production of

printed matter?

- Are the running costs as predicted?
- Has there been any identifiable shortfalls in the technology?
- Have all operating staff been properly trained?
- Do the operating and supervisory staff have any suggestions for improvement?
- Have there been any recent technology developments that might help expand the capabilities of the system to the benefit of the organisation?
- Does the system offer sufficient flexibility to produce the required artwork?
- Does the system offer sufficient typefaces, graphics and other elements for the new publications jobs that may have arisen since the initial feasibility study?
- Have there been any known software or hardware failures?
- What new applications has the system satisfied?

Using a checklist similar to the one above, it should be possible to determine whether the users of the desktop publishing technology are satisfied with the system and whether any organisational improvements need to be made, and to provide feedback on the effectiveness of the facility. This post implementation follow-up procedure should be carried out by a supervisor or manager, appointed to have overall responsibility for the activities (a publications manager, for example), and will involve managers of departments using the function either directly or indirectly.

REVIEWING RESPONSIBILITIES

In the chapter dealing with implementation, the subject of the siting of the desktop publishing system within the organisation was discussed. Where the system is originally located, in order to service the needs of the other departments, is also a matter for review. Any departments using desktop publishing directly, or relying on another department for a typesetting service, need to be periodically questioned about whether they feel that the resource is properly managed and available when required. Whoever is responsible for the management of the use of the resource may also be responsible for the budget for running costs, depreciation of equipment and future enhancement. Those departments who have a budget responsibility towards the desktop publishing system need to be measured for performance against budget; again, on a regular basis.

IMPLEMENTING A HOUSESTYLE

Using housestyles helps to keep consistency of standards, appearance and quality of output from desktop publishing systems within the organisation. The following give you an idea of the sort of things a housestyle document might include:

Page Size

Most desktop publishing systems allow the operator to select a variety of page sizes, including standard paper sizes and user-defined sizes. You may include a set of guidelines about paper sizes in the housestyle, such as A4 for reports and correspondence, A5 for price lists and brochures.

Running Headers/Footers

Are documents to contain running headers and footers for section headings, page numbers, and so on? If so, where are they to be located? Page numbers may be located, for example, at the foot of the page, centred, beneath hairline rules, etc.

Company Logos, Addresses, etc

How are these to be included on documents, if at all. You may want the organisation's name to appear on all public reports or, in cases where subsidiary companies are producing documents, for the holding company to be acknowledged within the layout.

Hyphenation

Hyphenation can be useful to prevent unnecessarily large spaces between words in justified text, or to reduce the degree of jagged edge you get with unjustified text. You may wish to stipulate whether to use hyphenation at all, particularly if you do not like the point where automatic hyphenation breaks words. If you wish to use discretionary hyphenation, the housestyle may be used to indicate to operators what hyphenation choices are acceptable.

Typefaces

Some organisations have a corporate typeface. This means they choose a typeface in which all company documentation is produced for the sake of identity or image. Other aspects of choosing typefaces might be to define when to use italics or bold (eg use italics for emphasising points within text, bold for headings only).

Graphics

If there are any general rules about the use of frames to surround pictures, headline rules, boxes around text, lines between columns, these can all be included as housestyle guidelines.

9 Finance and Cost Control

As any financial manager knows, the cost of acquisition of capital equipment such as a computer system, extends beyond the price tag on the equipment. The true cost must be measured in terms of the expenses involved in the selection process, training, installation, specialist staff recruitment and other such factors that can be ancillary to the main purchase, but when added together can easily exceed the capital outlay.

There are 'cheap' desktop publishing solutions: cheap software, low-cost 'compatible' computers and printers, but in real terms, once acquired, you find that there is much to spend money on in order to get the system working to your requirements. Cheap computers may be available, but they may be slow, and desktop publishing is the one software system that really needs processing speed. The software is hungry for computer memory, and for high-quality output, high quality printers do not come cheap. At the end of the day, a cheap solution does not remain cheap for long. There are a wealth of add-on costs for fonts, toner cartridges, memory boards, scanners, high resolution screens, a mouse, special operating systems, extra storage space, and a whole host of other accessories.

ACQUISITION COSTS

If you decide upon the purchase of a dedicated desktop publishing or special packaged system, you can at least expect that the price tag should cover all necessary components for the proper function and performance requirements of desktop publishing. It is much more difficult to assess the cost of a system when it is purchased in separate component parts, without specific quotes for all the known requirements.

So what kind of costs can one expect? This is almost impossible to answer. Prices, in any case, change so fast in the computer industry, though one thing you can be sure of is what you buy this week will be cheaper next week.

The following example illustrates a cost comparison between two systems for desktop publishing, based on prices at the time of publication, and which illustrate the difference between a PostScript and non-PostScript solution, both using standard, non-dedicated equipment:

PostScript Solution:

Apple Macintosh SE30 Micro including 40 Mbyte Hard Disk 2 MByte RAM 1 x 1.44 Mbyte Floppy Disk Drive Standard Keyboard and Mouse	2,750
Apple Laserwriter IINT PostScript Laser Printer (includes built-in fonts)	2,900
PageMaker software version 3.5	545
Total Cost	£6,195

Non-PostScript Solution:

Apricot Qi 350i 16MHz Micro (IBM PS/2 Compatible) including 47 Mbyte Hard Disk 2 MByte RAM 1 x 1.44 MByte Floppy Disk Drive	2,780
HP LaserJet Series II PCL Laser Printer	1,395
Microsoft Mouse	89
1 Mbyte Memory Upgrade for Laser Printer (for soft fonts and graphics)	259
Typographica Soft Fonts (standard collection)	86
Xerox Ventura Publisher	900
Total Cost	£5,509

The two systems illustrated above are not meant to be compared directly, though they both include computers of similar power and capacity, and software of repute. The additional costs of fonts and memory in the non-PostScript example are what one would probably consider fairly essential additions rather than optional extras.

In about a year's time from the date of publication of this book, you will probably be able to halve these prices for an equivalent computing facility.

Leasing offers an alternative to outright purchase. For equipment such as the computer and laser printer, the major components of the system, such as a 40 Mbyte 386 PC and an HP LaserJet, you are probably looking at around £15 per week each (excluding VAT) for a lease over three years (totalling £4,680) and then there is the cost of any software and accessories.

To rent or hire can be much more expensive. For example, an HP LaserJet could cost £62 per week, and a 386 microcomputer about £114 per week based on a 3 month rental.

Computer technology depreciates almost as fast as a second-hand car, if not faster. It is a case of technology quickly becoming redundant. Accountants are advised to write-down the value of the technology faster than other assets, and look for a return on capital employed within 12-18 months.

If you need hardware and software to provide a desktop publishing solution, another purchasing option is a DTP package, put together by suppliers as a complete system, including all the basic requirements, but as a cheaper option to buying the separate components.

For example:

Total DTP Packaged Solution

Including:

IBM compatible microcomputer
A4 paper white monitor
Mouse
Laser printer
Laser controller card
PageMaker or Ventura software
Cables
Starter consumables
1 year's on-site maintenance
Delivery

Total Cost: £4,750

Apart from the basic system, there are plenty of additional peripheral hardware devices to choose from to supplement the desktop publishing system. Again, prices vary widely, but some examples at the time of publication are shown below:

Graphics software:	
Gem Draw Plus	60
PC Paintbrush Plus	99
Flatbed desktop scanner	1,500
Hand held scanner	200
PostScript upgrade options for PCL printers:	
GoScript	200
HP JetScript	1,999
Pacific Page cartridge	549
Upright A4 paper white screen	550

OPERATING COSTS

Desktop publishing sells on the promise that the production of artwork internally can save costs. This is proposed on the basis that producing artwork for printed material can be an expensive exercise if traditional methods are used. So what are the costs involved in traditional methods?

Generally, it is regarded that if an organisation requires a printed document, the design and artwork production of that document are handled by an external service. This may be found at a printers, design studio, advertising agency or High Street quick-print shop, for example. Using the services of a designer to produce a layout for a publication, and the subsequent production of high-quality text (typesetting), can form a significant proportion of the total production cost of a publication:

cost to publish =

(cost to design) +
(cost to proof) +
(cost to typeset) +
(cost to alter) +
(cost to prepare artwork for printing) +
(cost of materials) +
(cost of printing) +
(cost of finishing)

In particular, the first five items can account for anything up to half the total cost, depending on the print process used and the quantity to be printed. Clearly, the more complex the publication, for example, use of colour, photographs, etc, the more expensive the total cost. The total cost can only be evaluated on the basis of the unit-cost considerations.

In order to assess whether your desktop publishing system is indeed saving costs, you will need to spend some time working out a costing formula for the system that you have implemented. Even then, one of the more difficult variables to equate is the cost saved by reducing the timescale with which publication artwork can be produced, but this is likely to be one of the major benefits of using desktop publishing. Proofing and amendment costs to even small parts of the job can be expensive, relative to the overall cost, when using outside resources, and these costs increase the nearer the job gets to being ready for printing. An amendment at the early stages of typesetting is cheaper to deal with than once camera-ready artwork is prepared.

Costs of desktop publishing jobs need to be calculated by including the following variables:

Total cost of materials, M =

For example:
(cost of paper/bromide) +
(cost of toner) +
(cost of chemicals (phototypesetting only))

Total cost of labour time as hourly rate, L =

(cost of operator salary) +
(cost of operator NI) +
(cost of operator expenses/overheads) +
(cost of equipment depreciation)
divided by (number of working/operating hours)

So that the cost of producing a particular job can be worked out as:

M + (L x number of hours on job)

The equation may also need to be expanded to include variables for indirect labour, such as any administrative and supervisory costs, or costs for individuals' time for proofing and editing if this is separately handled. However, for the purposes of cost comparisons with externally produced jobs, do not include costs that are incurred anyway, such as reading or editing proofs sent for checking, unless, in the case of an externally produced piece of artwork, a keyboard operator has had to rekey any text that would otherwise not be necessary by using a desktop publishing system.

Comparing these costs with the equivalent costs of a print job carried out using external resources, requires that detailed pricing breakdowns are available for the jobs concerned. You will also need to take care to make comparisons fair, by selecting jobs of a similar nature.

You will expect a print job that was previously phototypeset using a typesetting bureaux, to be more expensive than the same job produced using the desktop publishing software on a laser printer. The quality of the job will have been reduced by using the laser printer. However, if the production costs of the artwork have been significantly reduced *and* the finished result of the job is quite satisfactory for the purpose to which it is intended, then the cost reduction is quite valid, and can be considered as a direct saving on the bottom line.

An alternative way of costing the desktop publishing jobs is by page, rather than hour. This is especially useful if comparing costs of typesetting bureaux who generally charge either by the A4 page, or by the number of words processed. For example, you can expect to pay between £4 and £9 for an A4 page typeset by a bureaux if you supply the layout on disk. If you expect a typeset page to be produced from printed copy, ie the typesetter must rekey the words and produce the layout according to a rough, you can pay as much as £25 per page. Some bureaux will offer laser printer output as an alternative at anywhere between 20 and 80p per A4 page. The problem with costing per page is that it is difficult to compare costs with manually prepared artwork, ie artwork that has been pasted up on an art board using typeset text, screened photographs, hand-drawn graphics, etc. In such cases, the type of page layout (the complexity and number of elements included) can vary the price of artwork for a job so much compared to machine-produced page layouts. You can be safe in the knowledge that any page layout that you can produce with satisfactory quality on a page make-up system will be favourably cheaper than the cost of skilled paste-up artists and designers.

BUDGETS

Part of a cost control mechanism should include the measurement of actual costs against a budget. When first implementing desktop publishing, you will find it difficult to establish an accurate budget, but the results of a feasibility study may well have given some idea of the intended cost reductions by producing artwork in-house, and this is a good place to start cost control. It may be useful to break down budgets by job (see Figure 9.1), by department (see Figure 9.2) or type of work carried out using desktop publishing.

Type of Job	Budget	Actual
Reports		
Correspondence		
Manuals		
Brochures		
Newsletters		

Table 9.1 **Budget Table By Job**

Department	Budget	Actual
Sales		
Marketing		
Administration		
Training		
Production		
Accounts		

Table 9.2 Budget Table By Department

For either of the cases shown in Tables 9.1 and 9.2, you may have information relating to print and production costs of various jobs prior to the installation of desktop publishing. Use this information as a guide to the effectiveness of the installation, and as a measure to ensure that objectives and targets set during the original feasibility study have been achieved. You may also wish to measure the amount of use the facility is getting within the organisation. This can help to ascertain whether the system is under-used or over-stretched. If it is under-used, it may be that there are other applications for which desktop publishing can be utilised. If the system is over-used, various factors can be attributed to the circumstances:

- too high a workload (insufficient resources);
- operation too slow (do the staff need more training?);
- too many errors (again, more training for the staff?);
- work unsuitable for the system (requires large professional systems).

The availability of a desktop publishing resource may also depend upon whether you have a computer system dedicated to the production of artwork, or whether desktop publishing is a secondary function on a computer used for other purposes (such as word processing or accounting). If the system seems overloaded in these circumstances, you may consider purchasing equipment and employing dedicated staff for the publication requirements. To determine the utilisation of the desktop publishing resource, you need to establish the following control ratios:

$$\text{DTP Availability} = \frac{\text{DTP Available Time}}{\text{Total Machine Time}} \times 100$$

$$\text{DTP Utilisation} = \frac{\text{Actual DTP Usage}}{\text{DTP Availability}} \times 100$$

10 Summary and Action Plan

Desktop publishing has emerged as a major growth area in personal computing. Beginning with the introduction of revolutionary software on Apple computers, the extent of the market now is as diverse as that of familiar office productivity tools such as word processors and spreadsheets. Unlike other software packages, however, the popularity of desktop publishing has been responsible for the development of a wide range of specialised hardware designed with the desktop publishing installation in mind.

For managers of organisations looking to implement a desktop publishing solution, the choice is difficult. There are so many systems on the market, with varying capabilities and prices, that it is not clear to the novice which is the most appropriate for a particular set of tasks. Indeed, one cannot always be sure what can be achieved by obtaining a desktop publishing system until it is acquired. Once you have sampled the capabilities of a system – any system – you can make better judgements about the limitations, if they apply, and make adaptations and changes to the basic system.

ACTION PLAN

The approach to devising a suitable solution can be broken down into the following simple stages:

- obtain some background information on the subject;
- define targets and objectives (eg do you want to replace all artwork production with an in-house solution, or do you simply want a facility for improving reports and general document layouts?);

- carry out a feasibility study to ascertain whether the objectives can be met by current technology, within a set timescale and budget, and whether the system would be beneficial in all areas targeted;

- begin a selection procedure.

Each of these points is summarised in the following paragraphs.

Obtaining Background Information

In order to get further information about desktop publishing systems and their capabilities and functions, beyond the information given in this book, you can try one or more of the following sources of information and help:

1) Contact a local computer dealer for a demonstration of some software. The advantage of this approach is that you can begin to see what desktop publishing can do for real. The disadvantage is that, if you are just 'browsing' for further information, you may find the sales pressure from a computer dealer somewhat heavy.

2) Look for magazine articles in the computer press and reviews of desktop publishing software. This will help you to assimilate details of what various software packages can do, what kind of equipment they need to operate on and what sort of output quality they can achieve.

3) Having identified some suppliers of desktop publishing software, write to, or phone, the manufacturer (software house) for brochures on the product. Like magazine reviews, you will find out what suitable equipment is needed to run the various packages, and equally important, what output devices are supported.

4) Find out about computer exhibitions that are taking place, and whether there is likely to be any coverage for desktop publishing. If there is one at a convenient time and place, pay a visit for an information-gathering exercise. Don't expect to be able to make any purchasing decisions at such events – there is usually far too much to choose from at once. At best, you will come away with many free carrier bags full of sales literature.

5) Look out for information seminars on desktop publishing, run by independent organisations. These can be useful ways of learning about the pros and cons of various types of system, and often combine a small exhibition of a few systems for hands-on demonstrations. These also give you an opportunity of talking to those who have experience of several different systems.

6) If you already have a personal computer, you can try out some desktop publishing software at a very low cost using 'shareware'.

Shareware is very cheap demonstration software. You can buy it from shareware suppliers, who you will find advertising in almost any personal computing magazine. The cost of a disk can be about £5, but you get no manuals, and the program is often restricted in some way, so that it does not operate like the full version (for example, it may only permit small files to be stored). If you find that the program is of use, you can choose to register directly with the software producers to obtain manuals, technical support and the full software system. By adopting this approach you can either get a feel for desktop publishing and how it operates, or you can try out several packages, for very little cost, at your own leisure before choosing one for purchase.

Defining Targets and Objectives

This exercise should form part of a feasibility study for the implementation of desktop publishing. To summarise the points that require consideration:

- what type of publications are currently produced?
- for each of the above, define the type of publication: printed, photocopied, type of finishing, use of colour, graphics, etc;
- for each publication, list the current internal and external resources used to produce the publication, and who does what;
- try to identify what aspects of the production cycle of publications can be attributed to desktop publishing (original artwork for paste-up, graphics, camera-ready page make-up, printed, finished copies, etc);
- identify how much control you want over the various production elements (ie how much do you want the desktop publishing system to do, and for which publications);
- what new published material do you wish to be able to produce using desktop publishing?

Having gathered the above information, you should be able to define your objectives for the implementation of desktop publishing. Your objective may be a simple case of using DTP to create course notes, not currently produced at all, and you feel that the acquisition of desktop publishing system can be justified on this one requirement. Alternatively, you may require desktop publishing to replace your reliance on external services for existing publications. Either way you should then establish your equipment requirements:

- what kind of output device is necessary – laser printer or phototypesetter;

- if phototypesetting is required, can you cost justify the purchase or lease of such expensive equipment, or will a bureaux service provide a compromise?

- is PostScript necessary? What kind of output quality and facilities do you need for the publications you intend to produce?

- are there any special requirements in terms of graphics? Will a scanner provide your image processing requirements or do you need to cope with colour reproduction from transparencies?

By answering questions like those above, you should be able to determine whether the objectives are attainable.

Feasibility Study

This part of the process defines the responsibilities for the implementation and selection of the desktop publishing system, its distribution and use throughout the organisation, the budget, staff and training requirements of individuals involved.

Selection Process

Having gathered all previous information, it is possible to begin the task of selecting the software and hardware required to do the job.

SUMMARY OF OTHER POINTS

Here are a few points, some of which have been discussed generally throughout the book and some other additional considerations, that have been summarised here under main headings for assistance in decision making:

PCL and PostScript Options

There are laser printer standards that cause confusion among novices, and since the cost of the laser printer can be one of the most expensive components, the matter needs to be clear before making the decision one way or another.

The PCL language is that of Hewlett Packard's LaserJet printers, but is copied by many other laser printer manufacturers.

PostScript is a comprehensive and flexible page description language created by Adobe Systems.

One of the main differences between the two is in the handling of fonts. The PCL system operates using special control commands that instruct the printer about certain style aspects and positioning requirements. A control command for a particular font, for example, is sent to the printer from the software package and the name, style, size, etc must be resident in the printer in order to respond to the command. If the font cannot be located, or if the printer receives an unrecognisable command, it substitutes the font which is most similar to the one requested.

When a PostScript printer receives messages about fonts, all it needs is information about the outline – the shape of each character in the font. The page description language can then create any size and style of font from the outline when the document is sent to the printer for processing containing the requests for particular styles and sizes. PostScript printers can therefore handle multiple fonts more efficiently.

PCL printers can have many fonts available, but these often have to be stored externally to the printer, often on the computer's hard disk, and they take up a lot of room. If soft fonts are used (these are downloadable files containing font information) then a font file is required for every style *and* size that the printer is likely to require when printing a document.

PostScript printers produce font sizes and styles by making a kind of 'mathematical' transformation of the original outline, and this enables them to scale fonts to any size. They also have other advantages, relating to the way in which they can handle graphics more easily than PCL printers.

Making the choice between the two largely depends upon what you want to do. As a general guideline:

- if you intend to produce documents containing a good deal of graphic images, if you want a wide variety of fonts at different sizes and if you want to be able to scale the size of the output of your printed document – choose PostScript;

- if you want to send output to a phototypesetter, and perhaps proof material on a laser printer – choose PostScript;

- if you intend to set up a desktop publishing system requiring the use of professional electronic publishing software, because typesetting forms a major requirement in the organisation – choose PostScript;

- otherwise, choose a PCL printer.

If you choose a PCL printer and find that it is inadequate for your purposes, you can always upgrade to PostScript later. It might cost a little more than having bought a PostScript printer in the first place, but if you find that a PCL printer handles all you need, you can certainly save money in the first place.

Choosing the Computer

If you do not already have a microcomputer on which to run desktop publishing software, you can consider one of the following options:

- purchase a dedicated system such as the Xerox Documentor system;
- purchase a microcomputer;
- purchase a phototypesetting front-end.

In most cases, the choice will be to purchase a microcomputer unless the publishing facilities required by the organisation are extensive. If you do need to acquire a microcomputer you are advised to consider the following specification. It is not essential, and many packages will operate on a lesser configuration, which will cost less, but experience shows that the following features cause less frustration:

- the Apple Macintosh computers with a hard disk are all suitable candidates for desktop publishing (though they may not integrate with other computers that you have);
- for IBM PC-compatible computers choose one with a reasonable fixed (hard) disk of at least 20Mbytes;
- the faster the computer, the better. Ideally, choose a 80386 processor-based machine, running at at least 16 MHz;
- the minimum memory requirement should be 640 Kbytes, but ideally you should have access to extended memory of at least 1 Mbyte (some desktop publishing systems can use this extra memory for faster processing);
- ensure that the screen has at least EGA or MCGA capabilities (ask the supplier if in doubt), and if your budget can stretch to it, go for an A4 or A3 size screen;
- unless you are opting for a command/macro-based electronic publishing system, you will almost certainly need a mouse. Some computers are sold with a mouse as part of the package, but if not, there are plenty to choose from.

Do You Need Graphics Software?

Many desktop publishing systems provide the basic drawing tools for lines, boxes, circles and similar line functions. Some also offer some shading facilities for producing half-tone effects of various densities. Unless you intend to originate your own illustration material as well, these tools are usually adequate for the production of interesting and varied page layouts.

Graphics software packages can be useful for the production of simple illustrations. Flow charts, graphs, etc, can be produced using these packages and then included in a document layout. However, if you use a spreadsheet or database system, which can automatically generate graphs and charts, these can often be directly transferred into a page layout of a desktop publishing system, so that you do not have to redraw them.

Graphics software can produce some very good-looking illustrations, though many of the examples shown by the suppliers and within the documentation accompanying the software would be considerably time consuming to reproduce and require some considerable artistic skills on the part of the operator.

By far the best way to include graphics is to do one of the following:

- use a scanner to transfer an existing image, photograph, etc into the desktop publishing software;
- use a ready-drawn graphic – you can buy these in 'libraries' of picture files on disk, known as 'clip-art';
- provide space for the graphics in your layout, and have the image pasted into place afterwards (ie forget trying to create an electronic image).

Remember that although scanners are very useful supplements to the desktop publishing system, they cannot reproduce half-tones with the same quality as a screened photograph produced by a camera process. If high-quality photography is required in a document, you will need to seek the services of a printer or design studio.

Phototypesetting Using a Bureau Service

Where your publishing requirements extend to brochures, sales literature, corporate documents, etc, it is likely that the use of a laser printer will be unsatisfactory. The difference between the resolution of laser printers and phototypesetters is considerable, and if you think that waiting for the technology to catch up is all you need to do, think again. For one thing, there is a physical limitation to the resolution capabilities of a laser printer – partly to do with the paper, partly to do with the accuracy with which the paper can be transported through the printer, and partly to do which the physical limitation on the resolution capabilities of toner particles.

You could, on the other hand, wait for the price of phototypesetting to come down, whenever that may be. In the meantime, for many desktop publishing users, the alternative is to use the services of a bureau which has invested in a phototypesetting system. You can process files that you have created on your desktop publishing system, for a fee charged per number of words, pages or whatever.

Many bureaux can phototypeset document files generated on the various popular desktop publishing systems, particularly where the files are in PostScript format. Phototypesetters often have an extensive range of fonts available; in fact, font libraries for phototypesetters can extend to as many as 2,000 font families.

According to the speed of turnaround you want for a document, there are a number of ways you can approach the service. Here are a few choices:

- send a disk in the post and wait for the document to be processed, and the bromide output returned in the post;
- send the document to the bureau via a communications link (modem for example) and wait for the output to be posted back;
- send the document to the bureau via a communications link, and receive a proof back via the link, either on your computer screen or printed out on a fax machine. When the output is correct, process the job through the phototypesetter and wait for return of the bromides.

If you choose to use a bureau service, you should tighten up your proofing and editing cycles prior to processing. Once the document has been phototypeset by the bureau, author changes and layout amendments can be very expensive and can usually be avoided.

If phototypesetting is likely to be a major requirement, you might consider an option like the one offered by a company called Typeshare Limited*. For this you either purchase a special desktop publishing software package to run on a personal computer, or buy or hire a phototypesetting front end. Whichever hardware you choose, you are connected up to a phototypesetter via a communications link. You can typeset a page layout and send it to the phototypesetter via the communications link and, if you include a fax machine on the network, you can optionally receive back a proof of the artwork on the fax.

Once finalised, the actual job is then processed in a queue, and the bromide output posted to you. The cost of the service includes the price of the software or a front end typesetting machine, then the cost

*Typeshare Limited can be contacted by phoning 01 405 7937.

of processing time and materials and a line charge for the duration of the communications link-up.

Desktop Publishing and Colour

Desktop publishing can produce artwork for colour printing requirements. Some software packages enable elements of a page to be highlighted to indicate that they will ultimately be printed in a particular colour. When the page layout is printed out, the system prints separate sheets of camera-ready artwork for each of the colour separations, with registration marks to enable the printer to align the artwork properly for reproduction.

Achieving Your Objectives

With a little luck, as well as good judgement, you should be able to operate a smooth running desktop publishing system, that will be both beneficial to the organisation and inspirational for the users. In order to ensure it remains that way, remember the following:

- make sure your staff are properly trained;

- regularly check that the system is performing to expectations (cyclic review);

- ensure that the use of the system is properly managed – desktop publishing can so easily be subject to abuse;

- check the quality of output on a regular basis. If possible, have the advice of an experienced typographer or designer on good page layout, and to provide constructive criticism of your documents;

- check that your system is performing against budget. Try not to let the capital expenditure run away with itself, which is so easy to do when you add accessories to the system. If you, as a manager, are responsible for the expenditure on desktop publishing, be vigilant when your staff request add-ons to the system;

- finally, keep an eye on the desktop publishing market for new technology, trends towards particular solutions, and improvements in existing systems. You will have to keep up if you wish to avoid finding yourself with unsupported, out-of-date technology.

Appendix A
Glossary

The following are some of the terms associated with desktop publishing and typography that you may find useful.

Alignment

This refers to the position of text on a page or within a column. It may be aligned left (ranged to the left and ragged right), centred, aligned right (ranged right and ragged left) or justified (text lines up on both left and right). See also Quadding.

Anchor

A specific position on a page may be defined as an anchor point to which, for example, a graphic may be associated. So, if the layout of the page changes the graphic stays fixed to its specified anchor point.

Ascender

This is the part of a lower case letter that rises above its main body or x-height (see also x-height), with such letters as b, h and d. See also Descender.

Baseline

Different typefaces vary in size and style and, so that they can be mixed on the same line, are aligned on an imaginary horizontal reference line known as the baseline.

H H H H

Bit-mapping

This relates to the building up of an image using a matrix of dots. Scanners and laser printers use bit-mapping for processing graphics. The quality of the image produced is dependent upon the resolution or density of dots in a given area. This is usually expressed as a number of dots per inch; for example, 300 dpi.

Bleed

A graphic image may be placed on a page such that it extends beyond the page edge. If the document is reproduced by a commercial printer, the excess paper is cut off when the page is trimmed to size, and the graphic consequently extends to the very edge of the paper.

Bromide

This is the photosensitive paper on which the output of a phototypesetter is developed through a processor, not unlike a film processing system. In fact, the term 'film setting' is still used by some people, and the bromides are referred to as the film output.

Cicero

This is a unit of measure that is common in Europe. It is equivalent to 4.55 millimetres or 0.178 of an inch and is used for measuring type. See also Point System.

Clipboard

This is where text or graphics that have been 'cut' are temporarily stored by DTP systems. See also Cut and Paste.

Condensed Type

This is not often available on DTP systems and is found as a facility of some digital phototypesetters. The term itself refers to the relative narrowness of characters in a particular typeface. For a digital typesetter, changing what is known as the 'set width' can invoke the condensing of the characters. For example, a 14-point character can be defined as having a set width of 12 points, which reduces the size of the character's width rather than simply adjusting the space between the characters.

This is 14pt with normal set width
This is 14pt with a set width of 12pt

Crop Marks

These are the small lines that indicate the corners of a page when the page is smaller than the paper on which it is printed. They are used as guides for trimming the page to its correct size and may also be referred to as tick or trim marks.

Cut and Paste

This phrase, used often in DTP systems, describes the facility of 'cutting' a piece of text or graphics, therefore removing it from the page, and then 'pasting' it in another place. Before the advent of DTP and WYSIWYG screens this process used to be done manually, literally cutting and then pasting into position with adhesive.

Descender

This is the part of a lower-case character that hangs below its main body or x-height (see also x-height), with such letters as g, y and p. See also Ascender.

Discretionary Hyphen

This is a hyphen, placed in a word at an appropriate point, so that the system hyphenates the word if it does not fit properly at the end of the line. If the word does fit properly or, for example, more text is added which places the word on the following line anyway, the hyphen does not appear. See also Hyphenation.

Downloadable Fonts

These are fonts that are bought separately and installed, to increase the variety of typefaces that are available on the printer. They may also be referred to as 'soft' fonts.

Em Dash (—)

The size of this dash is the body width of the type size currently being used. It is used as a punctuation mark to break off one phrase from another where they do not flow naturally.

Em Space

See Fixed Spaces.

En Space

See Fixed Spaces.

Expanded Type

This is effectively the opposite to condensing type. For digital type-setters, altering the set width can cause the characters of a particular typeface to be expanded horizontally so as to occupy more width, for example, a 12-point character with a set width of 14 points.

This is 12pt with normal set width
This is 12pt with a set width of 14pt

Fixed Spaces

In typography, where certain fixed spaces between characters are required, a system of spacing based on points of space is employed to adjust the space between words or characters that is otherwise variable, depending upon the justification of the text on the line.

There are three commonly used spacings:

Em Space – generally, this is a space which is equivalent to the value of the point size, so that a 14-point em space will be 14 points wide.

En Space – this is half an em space.

Thin Space – this may be either one quarter or one third of an em space.

These spaces are used to make adjustments where additional fixed space is required, for example the first line of most of the paragraphs within this book are indented from the left-hand margin.

Folio

The folio is the page number, usually placed at the top or bottom of a page, which may be aligned right, centred or aligned left according to the page layout. See also Footer and Header.

Footer

This is usually a piece of information placed at the bottom of each page, though it may include a graphic, such as a line or logo, and it is often used to show such things as the page number, name of the publication, etc. It may also be called a trailer or running footer. See also Header.

Fount (Font)

A complete set of characters in the same typeface and size, including letters, punctuation and symbols. For example, 12pt Garamond is a different fount to 12pt Garamond italic, or 12pt Univers, etc.

Frame

A non-printing border which defines the limits of a column of text or graphic image on the page. When displayed on the screen as faint dotted lines, frames are particularly useful when working with multiple column documents to see where the limits of text and graphic column boundaries are in relation to one another.

Galley

The word 'galley' is generally only used in phototypesetting, since it refers to a continuous length of typeset material which may be used for proofing or cutting and pasting into position according to the layout requirements. Whereas DTP systems are designed to control the format and layout of the text before output, commercial typesetters would often provide the setting as lengths of text, set at the appropriate width. If this was then required for a manual, for example, the galleys would need to be cut to the size of the pages, in order to achieve the pagination and the text would be pasted into its correct position on the pages.

The term originates from the 'hot metal' process of typesetting, where a metal tray with raised edges was used to hold about 20 inches of metal type. In this context the term galley referred to the amount of text set, but the word is more generally used to define the status of a job, ie a job which has reached 'galley stage'. For example, in book publishing it is usual for a book to be set in galleys, then these are proofed back to the author for checking. Once the final setting alterations are made, the galley is turned into paginated or formatted output according to the design requirements of the job.

Graphics

Lines, ovals, rectangles, squares or circles created using the drawing tools of a DTP system are graphics. They may also be bit-mapped images, either created using the DTP system or imported from another application or scanner. See also Bit-mapping.

Greeking Text

When a page layout is reduced in size on the screen, often to facilitate the viewing of the full page area, the text may be represented as shaded blocks which exactly match the line breaks and position of the text. This may be necessary if the size of the text is too small at the reduced view to read legibly. Text displayed in this way is said to be 'greeked'.

Gutters

This refers to the space between columns in a multiple-column page layout.

Hairline

The thinnest possible rule (line), which is usually 0.25 of a point.

Half-tone

A printed illustration usually produced photographically, in which lights and shades of the original are represented by small and large dots, or varying concentrations of dots or lines.

Header

This is usually a piece of information placed at the top of each page, though it may include a graphic, such as a line or logo, and it is often used to show such things as the page number, name of the publication, chapter headings, etc. It may also be called a running header. See also Footer.

Hyphenation

This is the process of deciding where to hyphenate the last word on a line. Some systems will do this automatically, based on a hyphenation dictionary, but you may wish to override this and include your own. See also Discretionary Hyphen.

Icon

A small graphic image on the screen that represents a function, object or pointer tool. For example, the image of a pencil to represent the tool for drawing.

Indents

Space defined at either end of the line to change the placement of the text. The most common form of indent is for a paragraph denoting the beginning of a block of text. Generally, you should make the indent space proportional to the length of the line, for example:

lines under 24 picas wide	– indent 1 em space
lines between 25-36 picas wide	– indent 1½ em spaces
lines 37 picas wide or over	– indent 2 em spaces

Justified Text

Text that is aligned on both the left- and right-hand margins of the document, as used in this book.

Kerning

Kerning is the reduction of space between characters of a typeface in order to improve the appearance when certain pairs of characters appear together. For example, the letter W, when typeset, has a certain amount of optical space beneath the slant of the right and left downstrokes, and this can vary from typeface to typeface. If the letter following it, for example, is set with the normal letterspacing, it can appear to be displaced too far to the right. By subtracting points of space from between the characters, for example, the following letter effectively overlaps into the set width of the W, making the appropriate optical correction.

Paired kerning is the term used where a composition software system identifies the pairs of characters that require space adjustment and applies kerning automatically, provided the facility is switched on. Generally, the kerning requirement is more noticeable the larger the size of the typeface.

Leader

These are dots or dashes that fill the blank space left on a line, usually inserted automatically by the DTP system when specified. For example:

Chapter 1 ....Introduction

Leading

The amount of vertical space, expressed in points, between the baselines of two lines of text (it is pronounced 'ledding').

Letterspacing

This is the term that refers to the amount of space between individual letters, and on most phototypesetters is adjusted by subtracting or adding points of space. This is known as negative or positive letterspacing respectively. Positive letterspacing may be used to put space between the letters of words, rather than have larger gaps between the words themselves which might make them look spread along the line width. Sometimes, positive letterspacing may be used to achieve a particular effect, for example, to space out the characters of a heading.

Generally, positive letterspacing interrupts the legibility of the text, so negative letterspacing is the more commonly used adjustment. This is used to tighten the spacing between letters to improve the appearance of the text, adjust space for *kerning* or to fit copy into a tight space.

Macros

A term used to describe a simple function (perhaps a single or combination of keystrokes) which performs a series of much more complicated tasks, which are usually user-definable.

Mouse

A mouse-sized pointing device manipulated by hand on a desktop surface, which controls the movement of a cursor or pointer on the screen in relation to the movements of the mouse itself. It also has one to three buttons on the top which can invoke various functions or selections. A mouse may either mechanically or optically translate its movements into co-ordinates for the screen cursor. Optical mice require special surfaces on which to operate.

Page Description Language (PDL)

This is a software facility which is independent of the hardware of desktop publishing systems. It is used to convert a screen image which may include text and graphics, into instructions that can be used to drive an output device like a laser printer. Using such an independent interface allows control over text and graphics, and multiple typestyles and sizes. PostScript is probably one of the best known page description languages, and is generally regarded as the current standard. It has been adopted by a wide range of manufacturers, including IBM and Apple, and offers a path to phototypesetting from PC front ends. PostScript was developed by Adobe. Other PDLs include Xerox Interpress, Imagen Impress and Imagen/HP DDL.

Page Make-up Software

This is software that can produce 'compound documents' which can comprise text and graphics together. Using the concept of electronic paste-up, page make-up software can use text files generated on a word processor for pasting into a page layout. Graphics can be similarly imported or scanned in directly. Page make-up software normally uses a page description language. The distinction of such a package is that text-only software, such as a word processor, has limited output capabilities without a PDL, and provides limited control over layout and typefaces.

Pagination

Pagination is the process of assembling text, graphics, running headers, folios, etc to produce pages of the required length ready for printing. This can be done by cutting and pasting-up setting and illustrations, etc by hand, or electronically using a DTP or phototypesetting system.

Pica

A measurement equal to one sixteenth of an inch (see Point System).

Pi Characters/Founts

These are special characters or symbols such as ¼, ½, ¾, +, @, <, >, etc. They may be used for maths purposes or may simply be decorative.

Point System

A point is a unit of measurement generally considered to be equal to one seventy-second of an inch. However, there have been three point systems introduced:

The American-British system – point is measured as 0.1383 inch, or one twelfth of a pica (pica being 0.166 inch).

The Didot system – basic unit is the cicero, which is equal to 12 corps (points) or 0.178 inch. The Didot corps measures exactly 0.01483 inch.

The Mediaan system – point (or corps) measures 0.01374 inch. For general purposes, it is useful to remember: 6 picas to one inch, 72 points to one inch and 12 points to one pica. These, however, are not strictly accurate conversions since the point does not directly relate to inches.

Portrait/Landscape Format

Terms referring to the orientation of a page when printed. Portrait means that the page is printed so that the longest sides are vertical (like the pages of this book); landscape is such that the sides of the page are the shortest.

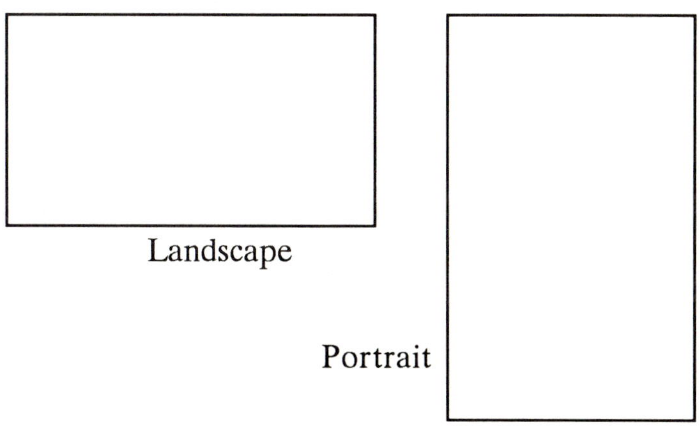

Proportional Spacing

Spacing between individual characters such that each character has an amount of horizontal space on the line proportional to the width of the character itself. For example, the letter i will need much less space than the letter m.

Quadding

A term relating to the placement of text. The word originates from 'quadrat', which was a metal cube used for filling blank spaces in hand typesetting. Quads, therefore, are used to specify where the remaining space on a line is to be positioned.

This is quad left

This is quad right

This is quad centre

Raster Image Processing

This device is the basis of truly controllable desktop publishing. It converts instructions into a bit map (see Bit Mapping) and allows a laser or page printer to use a page description language (see Page Description Language).

Roman

Ordinary letters, as distinct from italic, bold, etc.

Rules

A term used in printing and design to refer to horizontal or vertical lines; for example, as used in forms.

Serif/Sans Serif

Serifs are the short lines drawn at right angles to, or obliquely across, the ends of stems and arms of letters. The term is also used to describe typefaces that have this feature (eg Times). Sans serif is a typeface without serifs (eg Helvetica).

Set Width

The set width of a character relates to its point size, so a 9pt character has a set width of 9. Some typefaces, however, are designed with a narrower set width, eg 9pt with 8.5 set width.

Small Caps

These are capital letters designed to match the x-height of a typeface, though many founts these days do not have small caps so they are created by reducing the point size to 80% of its original size. They are used for abbreviations of awards, titles, etc following a name, or where whole words in text are set in all caps.

CAPS and SMALL CAPS

Soft Fonts

See Downloadable Fonts.

Style Sheet

All the styles that describe the design of a publication's layout and typefaces stored as a group, either in a file format or associated with a macro (see Macro).

Superior/Inferior Characters

These terms relate to characters usually set in a smaller size to the text typeface, and positioned above (superior) or below (inferior) the baseline. They are often referred to in DTP systems as superscripts and subscripts respectively.

$A^2 \quad B_4$

Tags

Labels given to paragraphs and other elements of a document which relate to a particular set of formatting instructions. For example, a paragraph tag may relate to the instructions that define the typeface, size, line length, spacing and other attributes.

Tick Marks

The small lines used by printers as guides for trimming a page to size (see also Crop Marks).

Template

Actually a style sheet but often used as a model layout for similar publications (see Style Sheet).

Type Size

Type sizes are described by the basic unit of measurement, the point. Points are used to define the length of a metal block or chunk of type. The length of the metal block's top surface relates to the point or type size, though the character cast onto the surface will be smaller than the overall size of the metal. Traditionally, then, the point size of a typeface refers to the dimension of the metal block, not the height of the image. This is to allow room for the ascenders and descenders. Thus the type size relates to the distance between the top of the ascender and the bottom of the descender of the typeface.

Typography

The design of printed matter. A typographer is one who is responsible for the character and appearance of printed matter.

Vector Processing

The means by which typesetters use line segments or 'vectors' to outline a character by connecting the dots which are used as the basic building blocks of the character's shape.

Weight

The weight of a typeface varies according to its design. The thickness of line will determine how light or dark its image will appear after printing. There are standard terms for the various weights of a typeface and these are referred to as extralight, light, semilight, regular, medium, semibold, bold, extrabold and ultrabold. However, these variations are not standard across all typefaces. For example, 'medium' weight of one typeface may be the same weight as 'bold' in another.

Widows and Orphans

An orphan is the term used to describe the first line of a paragraph at the foot of a page when it is separated from the remainder which may be on the following page. A widow is the term used to describe the last line of a paragraph which appears at the top of a page, separated from the remainder which may be on the previous page.

Word Spacing

In phototypesetting the space between words is variable (unlike a typewriter), which enables lines of text to be justified. It also allows for the optimum number of words to be set on the specified line length.

WYSIWIG

(W)hat (Y)ou (S)ee (I)s (W)hat (Y)ou (G)et. This term is used to describe a feature of word processors or desktop publishing software systems that can represent on the screen display what the actual output of the document will look like. The degree of accuracy in this respect, however, varies greatly from system to system.

x-Height

This is the height of the letter x and is used to describe the height of the body of lower case characters in a particular typeface.

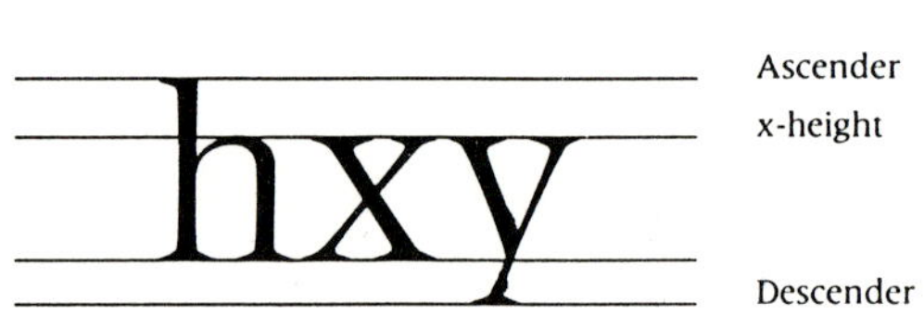

A change in x-height can affect the apparent size of typefaces that are actually the same size.

This has a tall x-height — set in 12pt Benguiat

This has a low x-height — set in 12pt Palacio

Zooming

The act of enlarging or reducing the view of a page layout. Enlarging the view of a portion of the document helps when working on detailed items, reducing the view allows the whole page or a pair of pages to be seen in full on the screen to check the overall appearance of the layout.

Also the facility to be able to change the output size of a document, at the time of printing, for PostScript-controlled devices.

Appendix B
Reference Material

The following pages contain some additional reference material relating to the following topics:

- Training
- Reviews
    - 3B2
    - Ventura Publisher
    - PageMaker
- Magazines
- Ways to Upgrade to PostScript
    - Software
    - Hardware
- UK User Groups
- Graphics File Formats
- Soft Fonts for PCL Printers

TRAINING

There are now a number of available independent training courses on desktop publishing systems and software. In addition to the seminars and courses, for those organisations already using desktop publishing, there are video-based training aids for the popular desktop publishing software. If you have the appropriate software, you may be able to obtain an operator video training package which gives guidance on the basics of operating the software. Your best source of information about whether a training package is available, is by direct correspondence with the software suppliers.

The software suppliers often have information about organisations known to them who offer training on their particular packages. Where possible, you should try to find training that covers a wide range of basic principles of desktop publishing as well as the specific facilities of a certain product. You may find that you wish to change your software at a later date, for more comprehensive facilities, in which case you will want to avoid retraining unnecessarily.

For details about training courses and seminars on desktop publishing, from independent sources, look through the computer press advertisements, and ask your local software and hardware retailer for details about training courses run for desktop publishing systems. Also ask your local business enterprise centre about computer based training courses. They may know of companies and training establishments in your area, who may be able to help you.

REVIEWS

The following three reviews offer a brief overview of three of the better-quality, and most popular desktop publishing systems currently available. They have been chosen because they are widely known and popular choices (PageMaker and Ventura) and because they offer a comprehensive set of features, particularly suitable for most desktop publishing requirements, regardless of the application (especially 3B2).

3B2

The system offers an integrated suite of software that can be used on a variety of different hardware and operating systems. With built-in word processor facilities, something not generally available in desktop publishing software, the user has a text entry facility which is supplemented by a set of tools for the production of graphics.

The system comes with a choice of page make-up interfaces. Either the mouse-based interactive WYSIWYG screen, using pull-down menus, dialogue boxes, etc, or by using a command-based interface with macros, better suited for professionals, which does not utilise the mouse interface at all.

Typesetting is achieved using Monotype typefaces, for both screen and output presentation, and the output device can either be a PostScript laser printer or phototypesetter.

Ventura Publisher

This desktop publishing system remains one of the biggest selling packages for the PC. It will operate on IBM compatible computers and the Xerox 6065.

The system uses a WYSIWYG interface with a mouse, and has no command-only driven interface option like 3B2.

It offers a wide range of typographical facilities for control of layouts, but it is suited best to the formatting of text files which have been 'tagged' and imported from word processors. To produce a complex page layout, such as a newsletter, as a one-off document can be a cumbersome task, and would take a novice user some considerable time to master. This is despite a professional extension option for the package, designed to extend the facilities of the software for more layout control of documents. Ventura is popularly used for large documents such as technical manuals. By setting up the style sheet first, then tagging the word processor files, a whole manual can be generated in one pass. If you want to make slight adjustments to line spacing, type size, indentation, etc, for just one paragraph, you will need to set up a new paragraph style.

The program operates on the basis of storing each piece of text or graphics in a frame. Frames can be resized and manipulated within the page area, though specially generated frames for headers and footers cannot be repositioned in respect of the margins of the paper. Unlike 3B2, Ventura is not suitable as an initial text entry facility for any document over one page long, and therefore relies upon the ability to import text from a variety of word processors.

The software will output documents on dot matrix printers, PCL laser printers, PostScript laser printers and Linotronic and Compugraphic phototypesetters. For PCL laser printers, the package includes soft fonts for Swiss, Dutch, Courier and Symbol typefaces.

PageMaker

PageMaker is a desktop publishing page make-up system for either the Apple Macintosh series computers, or the IBM PC and compatibles.

A powerful system operating within the Microsoft Windows environment on PCs, the system benefits from being used on a fast computer, perhaps more than most other DTP software, since operation is disk intensive. Like Ventura, PageMaker relies upon mouse-based WYSIWYG interface.

The page make-up process uses the analogy of a pasteboard, on which the text and graphics elements can be arranged. Its comprehensive range of typographical features give it a little more artistic flair than other desktop publishing systems, and for complex or one-off publications, newspaper and magazine style production, PageMaker is far simpler to control than Ventura. For long document production, PageMaker can handle publications of up to 128 pages (as opposed to Ventura's 999), and would be adequate for most purposes, though the system lacks the long document production features of Ventura, such as automatically taking section headings as input for running headers/footers and contents and index creation.

PageMaker will output to a variety of devices including PCL laser printers and PostScript printers, including phototypesetters such as the Linotronic Imagesetter.

For PCL laser printers, the PageMaker package includes Bitstream fontware for Swiss, Dutch, Courier and Symbol typefaces.

MAGAZINES

Many of the computer magazines currently on the stands at most newsagents, include suppliers' advertisements for desktop publishing software and hardware. Many magazines also feature particular products and include reviews of desktop publishing solutions, news, information and helpful tips. For publications specifically related to desktop publishing, including case studies of successful desktop publishing applications, contact:

DTP Desktop Publishing
Dennis Publishing Ltd
14 Rathbone Place
London W1P 1DE

Telephone 01 631 1433

WAYS TO UPGRADE TO POSTSCRIPT

If you use a PCL laser printer for desktop publishing output, such as a Hewlett Packard LaserJet or one of the many compatible printers, and you wish to upgrade to producing PostScript output, there are a number of ways you can achieve this, apart from buying a new PostScript laser printer:

Software

One of the popular facilities is called GoScript. This prints PostScript language text and graphics on laser, ink jet and dot matrix printers.

For less than £200, the basic version offers 13 fonts which are compatible with the Apple Laserwriter fonts. Like all PostScript fonts, they are scaleable and can be rotated to any angle. For a little more than £300, you can buy GoScript plus which has 35 fonts included.

The system requirements are IBM PC/XT/AT or compatible or PS/2 using the PC/MS-DOS operating system of at least version 3.0. Your PC will need a minimum of 640K memory and a hard disk.

The output can be produced on HP LaserJets and compatibles, but these must have at least 1 Mbyte of memory.

This is a remarkably cheap way of adding a PostScript facility, though it is slow to process. It is not recommended as a suitable facility for professional publication production, where performance is of paramount importance, but may be of benefit if the PostScript capability is only occasionally required.

Hardware

There are a couple of hardware-orientated options for upgrading. One of these is produced by Hewlett Packard for users of their LaserJet PCL printers. This product is called JetScript, and comprises a board which slots inside the computer and an adaptor for the laser printer. The system is a reliable way of upgrading the PCL printer, though the cost of it can be as much as the original cost of the laser printer.

An alternative is a cartridge device produced by Pacific Data Euro called Pacific Page. This is a PostScript emulation cartridge for the HP LaserJet Series II. The product supports PostScript output from widely available DTP and word processing programs, including Ventura Publisher and PageMaker, Word Perfect 5 and Microsoft Word. It includes 35 scaleable fonts plus all the usual text manipulation facilities of PostScript. The cartridge plugs into the HP LaserJet's cartridge slot so no additional boards or cables are required. It costs in the region of £550 including a year's warranty.

UK USER GROUPS

Some desktop publishing packages, such as PageMaker and Ventura, have their own dedicated user groups, whose members exchange tips and practical information regarding the everyday use of the product. These user groups may also be a useful source of information on the products for prospective purchasers.

The PageMaker User Group is located at:

PO Box 43
Newbury
Berkshire
RG1 4WH

Telephone: 0233 83571

The Ventura Publisher User Group is located at:

Apartment 22
36 Kingswood Drive
Sutton
Surrey
SM2 5NB

Telephone: 01 642 4118

GRAPHICS FILE FORMATS

Most desktop publishing page make-up software programs provide ways of importing drawings and scanned images from other software packages, or from files generated by scanner devices. Unlike text files, which tend to be stored in a much more straightforward manner, graphics files are often stored in a complex, coded format. Different types of system generate different file formats and these are identified by their file extension – often a three character mnemonic which describes the source of the document and the type of format in which the information is saved. The common graphics file formats are listed below with the graphics packages which generate them:

File format	Source graphics application/description
CUT	Dr Halo II
DXF	AutoCAD files
EPS	Aldus FreeHand and Adobe Illustrator
GIF	Compuserve graphics interchange format
IFF	Amiga graphics files
IMG	Gem image
MSP	Microsoft Windows Paint
PCX	PC Paintbrush
PIC	Lotus and PostScript formats, PC Paint
PNT	Macintosh MacPaint
TIF	Tagged Image File format
CGM	Lotus Freelance
GEM	Gem line art

SOFT FONTS FOR PCL PRINTERS

What fonts you need for desktop publishing depends upon the type of publication you are creating. For most applications, two or perhaps three fonts are probably all you will need – a serif for text and a sans serif for headings, notices, slides, etc.

PCL fonts contain all of the characters that share the same point size, type style and family in a file. They are also stored as either portrait or landscape format (see glossary). Fonts not resident in the laser printer can either be added by means of a plug-in cartridge (so that they 'become' resident as far as the printer is concerned) or downloaded from the computer when they are needed (soft fonts). Soft fonts can be purchased from independent suppliers and stored on the computer's hard disk. You can select from quite a range, and some suppliers, notably Typographica, offer sets of font families as a package. Soft fonts cause document production to be slower than resident fonts, and require quite a lot of disk space, so they tend to be installed to suit minimum requirements.

Soft fonts can be obtained from most desktop publishing system retailers. Suppliers of PCL fonts include:

Bitstream Fonts:

Microrite
Arena House
66-68 Pentonville Road
London N1 9HS

or

Bitstream Inc.
Athenaeum House
215 First Street
Cambridge
Massachusetts 02142
USA

Typographica:

GST Software Products Limited
The Moathouse
Melbourn Science Park
Melbourn
Cambridge
SG8 6EJ

Appendix C
Examples of Desktop Publishing Output

The following pages illustrate examples of publications and documents produced using desktop publishing. More than one type of system has been used, though they could all have produced the same results in this particular case.

Acme Corp.

Leaders in Industrial Innovation
123 Sapporro Road
Palos Verdes, CA 90274
(555) 541-1234

FOR IMMEDIATE RELEASE

For more information:
Mr. Joe Flack
(212) 555-1212

XYZ Corp. Ships 1000th Product

LOS ANGELES, CA, July 17 – XYZ Corp., the leading manufacturer of widgets for the automated widget supply industry, announced that it has shipped its 1000th Model 123-X enhanced widget. The customer is ABC Inc. of Livonia Hills, MI.

"This is an important step for XYZ Corp., and the emerging widget industry" said Joe Bloggs, president of XYZ Corp., "we have shipped more widgets than the other ten companies combined. We believe our technology is second to none."

Marketing plans, availability and pricing for the new widget line will be announced later this fall.

XYZ Corp. was formed in 1975. Headquarters are in Los Angeles, California.

Acme Corp.

Leaders in Industrial Innovation
123 Sapporro Road
Palos Verdes, CA 90274
(555) 541-1234

Mr. J. Smith
123 Main St.
Detroit, MI 98989

November 15, 1989

Dear Mr. Smith,

It has been called to our attention that you have been having a difficult time with our new widget. Upon reviewing your case, we found that you have failed to plug your widget into an electrical outlet. As you may know, out widget does require power to operate properly.

Thank you for buying our widgets, and we look forward to your continued business.

Sincerely,

Letter Head/Mailshot

BULLETIN*NEWS*

TechTile joins the desktop publishing revolution

To make all the company's materials look their best, TechTile Industries has always used state-of-the-art technology for business communications. Over the years, we have moved from manual to electric typewriters, then to centralized word-processing centers. During the past three years, every office worker from clerical to manager has been given the option of equipping his or her desk with a personal computer and various software packages for word-processing, spreadsheets, graphics, and electronic mail.

Now, TechTile Industries advances beyond letter-quality word-processing to typeset-quality desktop publishing. As a result, every employee can use personal computers to create more effective printed communications on the job.

Desktop publishing combines personal computers, high-quality printers that produce typeset-looking pages, and specialized page layout software. With this three-part system, you can combine word-processed text and computer graphics to design and print professional-looking documents without leaving your desk.

To make desktop publishing available to all employees immediately, TechTile Industries is adding desktop publishing workstations to every department in the company. These workstations will be in place only until we can install a desktop publishing system on every employee's desk.

TechTile Industries' Corporate Communications division has prepared this style guide to help you make the most of desktop publishing. *Desktop Publishing With Style* covers guidelines you should follow to:

- create the text and graphics to be included in your publications
- use page layout software to combine your text and graphics files into publications
- whenever possible, use the existing page designs in our company template package to create materials for external use
- if necessary, put in a request for desktop publishing training through the Personal Computing Division

Because desktop publishing offers tremendous flexibility, this section details style guidelines established by TechTile Industries' Corporate Communications division. Everyone should follow these guidelines so all company publications look consistent with each other and with the overall corporate image.

Setting up temporary workstations for document production

All letters, presentation overheads, reports, and other communications intended for distribution outside TechTile Industries can be produced at the temporary departmental workstations.

First priority for the workstations will go to people producing external documents. As available, the workstations can be used for internal communications, too.

Newsletter

Lorem Ipsum

Chapter 1

Lorem Ipsum

Lorem ipsum dolor sit amet, consectetuer adipiscing elit, sed diam nonummy nibh euismod tincidunt ut laoreet dolore magna aliquam erat volutpat. Ut wisi enim ad minim veniam, quis nostrud exerci tation ullamcorper suscipit lobortis nisl ut aliquip ex ea commodo consequat.

Duis Autem

Vel eum iriure dolor in hendrerit in vulputate velit esse molestie consequat, vel illum dolore eu feugiat nulla facilisis at vero eros et accumsan et iusto odio dignissim qui blandit praesent luptatum zzril delenit augue duis dolore te feugait nulla facilisi.

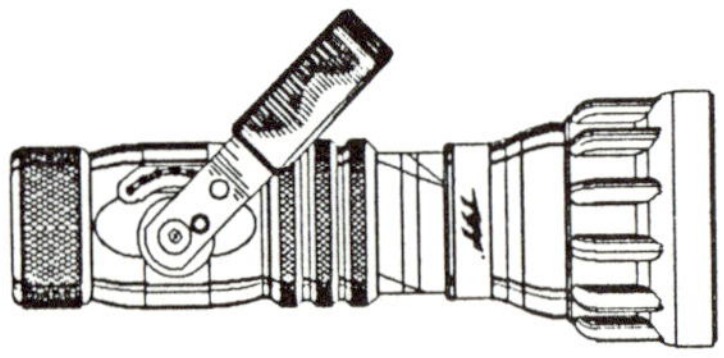

Lorem ipsum dolor sit amet, consectetuer adipiscing elit, sed diam nonummy nibh euismod tincidunt ut laoreet dolore magna aliquam erat volutpat. Ut wisi enim ad minim veniam, quis nostrud exerci tation ullamcorper suscipit lobortis nisl ut aliquip ex ea commodo consequat. Duis autem vel eum iriure dolor in hendrerit in vulputate velit esse molestie consequat, vel illum dolore eu

Technical Book

Company name

Address
Address
Address

Telephone
Telephone

Product Specs Headline

Subhead

Lorem ipsum dolor sit amet, consectetuer adipiscing elit, sed diam nonummy nibh euismod tincidunt ut laoreet dolore magna aliquam erat volutpat. Ut enim ad minim veniam, quis nostrud exerci tation ullamcorper suscipit lobortis nisl ut aliquip ex ea commodo consequat.

Duis autem vel eum irure dolor in hendrerit in vulputate velit esse molestie consequat, vel illum dolore eu feugiat nulla facilisis at vero eros et accumsan et iusto odio magna aliquam erat volutpat. Lorem ipsum dolor sit amet.

LIST HEADING

- List entry
- List entry
- List entry
- List entry
- List entry
- List entry
- List entry

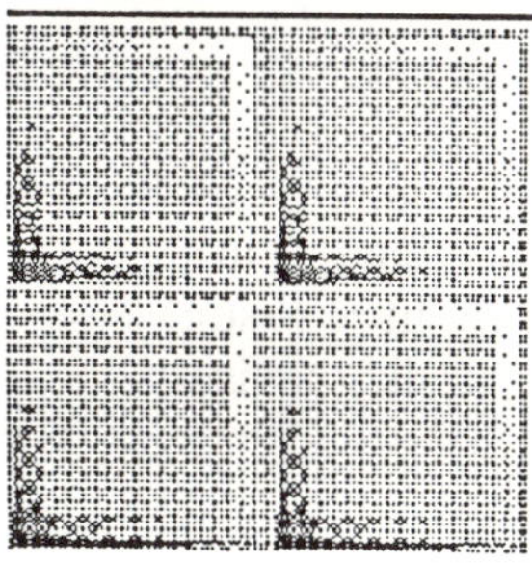

Subhead

Lorem ipsum dolor sit amet, consectetuer adipiscing elit, sed diam nonummy nibh euismod tincidunt ut laoreet dolore magna aliquam erat volutpat. Ut enim ad minim veniam, quis nostrud exerci tation ullamcorper suscipit lobortis nisl ut aliquip ex ea commodo consequat.

Duis autem vel eum irure dolor in hendrerit in vulputate velit esse molestie consequat, vel illum dolore eu feugiat nulla facilisis at vero eros et accumsan et iusto odio magna aliquam erat volutpat. Lorem ipsum dolor sit amet.

LIST HEADING

- List entry
- List entry
- List entry
- List entry
- List entry
- List entry
- List entry

Subhead

Lorem ipsum dolor sit amet, consectetuer adipiscing elit, sed diam nonummy nibh euismod tincidunt ut laoreet dolore magna aliquam erat volutpat. Ut enim ad minim veniam, quis nostrud exerci tation ullamcorper suscipit lobortis nisl ut aliquip ex ea commodo consequat.

Duis autem vel eum irure dolor in hendrerit in vulputate velit esse molestie consequat, vel illum dolore

Subhead

Lorem ipsum dolor sit amet, consectetuer adipiscing el:t, sed diam nonummy nibh euismod tincidunt ut laoreet dolore magna aliquam erat volutpat. Ut enim ad minim veniam, quis nostrud exerci tation ullamcorper suscipit lobortis nisl ut aliquip ex ea commodo consequat.

Duis autem vel eum irure dolor in hendrerit in vulputate velit esse molestie consequat, vel illum dolore

Subhead

Lorem ipsum dolor sit amet, consectetuer adipiscing elit, sed diam nonummy nibh euismod tincidunt ut laoreet dolore magna aliquam erat volutpat. Ut enim ad minim veniam, quis nostrud exerci tation ullamcorper suscipit lobortis nisl ut aliquip ex ea commodo consequat.

Duis autem vel eum irure dolor in hendrerit in vulputate velit esse molestie consequat, vel illum dolore

Footer Page 1

Product Specification

Centre Technologies Inc.

Computer Solutions for Publishing

2004 Curtis Ave. #A Redondo Beach, CA 90278 (213) 376-5724

March 1, 1990

Mr. Joe Smith
ABC Corporation
123 Main Street
Detroit, MI 43434

INVOICE

Quantity	Description	Price	Subtotal
1	Micromouse	$125.00	$125.00
5	Diskette boxes	$ 12.50	$ 62.50
1	Media-clean	$ 10.25	$ 10.25

Total now due $197.75

Please pay promptly within 30 days

Despatch date ____ *Carrier* ____

Received by ____ *GDN* ____

Invoice

Company name

Price List

Month 00, 0000

Product name	Description	Part number	Price
Lorem ipsum	Ullam corper suscipit lobortis nis Duis autem vel eum iriure	XXXXXX	£XXX.XX
Lorem ipsum	Ullam corper suscipit lobortis nis Duis autem vel eum iriure	XXXXXX	£XXX.XX
Lorem ipsum	Ullam corper suscipit lobortis nis Duis autem vel eum iriure	XXXXXX	£XXX.XX
Lorem ipsum	Ullam corper suscipit lobortis nis Duis autem vel eum iriure	XXXXXX	£XXX.XX
Lorem ipsum	Ullam corper suscipit lobortis nis Duis autem vel eum iriure	XXXXXX	£XXX.XX
Lorem ipsum	Ullam corper suscipit lobortis nis Duis autem vel eum iriure	XXXXXX	£XXX.XX
Lorem ipsum	Ullam corper suscipit lobortis nis Duis autem vel eum iriure	XXXXXX	£XXX.XX
Lorem ipsum	Ullam corper suscipit lobortis nis Duis autem vel eum iriure	XXXXXX	£XXX.XX
Lorem ipsum	Ullam corper suscipit lobortis nis Duis autem vel eum iriure	XXXXXX	£XXX.XX
Lorem ipsum	Ullam corper suscipit lobortis nis Duis autem vel eum iriure	XXXXXX	£XXX.XX
Lorem ipsum	Ullam corper suscipit lobortis nis Duis autem vel eum iriure	XXXXXX	£XXX.XX
Lorem ipsum	Ullam corper suscipit lobortis nis Duis autem vel eum iriure	XXXXXX	£XXX.XX

1

Price List

Company name placeholder Date placeholder

Memo

From: J P Geoffreys

To: H. D. Goodman

Re: Lorem Ipsum

Lorem ipsum dolor sit amet, consectetuer adipiscing elit, sed diam nonummy nibh euismod tincidunt ut laoreet dolore magna aliquam erat volutpat. Ut wisi enim ad minim veniam, quis nostrud exerci tation ullamcorper suscipit lobortis nisl ut aliquip ex ea commodo consequat.

Duis autem vel eum iriure dolor in hendrerit in vulputate velit esse molestie consequat, vel illum dolore eu feugiat nulla facilisis at vero eros et accumsan et iusto odio dignissim qui blandit praesent luptatum zzril delenit augue duis dolore te feugait nulla facilisi.

Lorem ipsum dolor sit amet, consectetuer adipiscing elit, sed diam nonummy nibh euismod tincidunt ut laoreet dolore magna aliquam erat volutpat.

Ut wisi enim ad minim veniam, quis nostrud exerci tation ullamcorper suscipit lobortis nisl ut aliquip ex ea commodo consequat. Duis autem vel eum iriure dolor in hendrerit in vulputate velit esse molestie consequat, vel illum dolore eu feugiat nulla facilisis at vero eros et accumsan et iusto odio dignissim qui blandit praesent luptatum zzril delenit augue duis dolore te feugait nulla facilisi.

Nam liber tempor cum soluta nobis eleifend option congue nihil imperdiet doming id quod mazim placerat facer possim assum.

Lorem ipsum dolor sit amet, consectetuer adipiscing elit, sed diam nonummy nibh euismod tincidunt ut laoreet dolore magna aliquam erat volutpat. Ut wisi enim ad minim veniam, quis nostrud exerci tation ullamcorper suscipit lobortis nisl ut aliquip ex ea commodo consequat. Duis autem vel eum iriure dolor in hendrerit in vulputate velit esse molestie consequat, vel illum dolore eu feugiat nulla facilisis at vero eros et accumsan et iusto odio dignissim qui blandit praesent luptatum zzril delenit augue duis dolore te feugait nulla facilisi. Lorem ipsum dolor sit amet, consectetuer adipiscing elit, sed diam nonummy nibh euismod tincidunt ut laoreet dolore magna aliquam erat volutpat.

Memo

MENU COMMANDS PUBLISHING CHAPTER

PUBLISHING CHAPTER

MENU COMMANDS

Most of Ventura Publisher's functions are controlled through the menus at the top of the screen. This section describes the operation of each of these menus and the options within them. These commands are presented in the order in which they appear on the screen. Use the index for an alphabetical reference to these commands.

Menu Conventions

Often, a menu option will be shown in gray and cannot be highlighted. This usually indicates that the proper function has not been selected. The table below indicates these dependencies.

DESK

Publisher Info . . .	Always available

FILE

New	Must first Open chapter or Load file
Open . . .	Always available
Save	File name must be in title bar
Save As . . .	Always available

FILE MENU

Description/Application

The File Menu controls information flow into and out of Ventura Publisher.

REFERENCE GUIDE 1-1

Technical Manual

Greenough's Directory

AST Research Inc.	(555) 863 1333
Abaton Technology	(555) 905 9399
Addison-Wesley Publishing Co.	(555) 944 3700
Adobe Systems Inc.	(555) 852 0271
Adserve Media Systems, Inc.	(555) 213 5700
Advanced Technologies Int'l	(555) 748 1688
AFIPS	(555) 620 8926
Airus	(555) 684 3000
Allied Linotype	(555) 434 2000
Allotype Typographics	(555) 577 3035
Alpha Software Corp.	(555) 229 2924
AlphaGraphics	(555) 882 4100
Altertext	(555) 426 0009
American Business Press	(555) 661 6360
Amgraf, Inc.	(555) 474 4797
Amrron Data Services	(555) 859 8333
Apple Computer, Inc.	(555) 996 1010
Applied Publishing Technologies	(555) 872 1190
Archtype	(555) 482 2739
Arrix Logic Systems Inc.	(555) 292 6425
Ashton-Tate	(555) 329 8000
AST Research Inc.	(555) 863 1333
Autographix	(555) 890 8558
Autologic	(555) 498 9611
Automatic Fulfillment Services	(555) 366 8722
Autospec Inc.	(555) 649 0890
Award Software Inc.	(555) 395 2773
Beach Media Inc.	(555) 226 6726
Bell & Howell Company	(555) 262 1600
BPAA	(555) 661 0222
Business Systems International	(555) 998 7227
Buttonware Inc.	(555) 746 4296
Canon USA Inc., Printer Div.	(555) 488 6700
Capital Equipment Co.	(555) 829 6220
Cauzin Systems, Inc.	(555) 573 0150
Centram Systems West, Inc.	(555) 644 8244
CF Inc.	(555) 829 4990
Chorus Data Systems	(555) 424 2900
Comm Type Interface Typesetting	(555) 938 8973
Composition Technology Intl.	(555) 848 1010
Compugraphic Corp.	(555) 944 6555
CompuNews, Inc.	(555) 826 1110
CompuScan, Inc.	(555) 288 6001
CompuServe	(555) 457 8600
Computer EdiType Systems	(555) 222 8148
Computing Software Services Inc.	(555) 432 6077
Concept Technologies, Inc.	(555) 684 3314
Creative Strategies Resrch Inter	(555) 249 7550
Cybertext Corp.	(555) 822 7079
Data Transforms	(555) 832 1501

Directory

WHEN YOU NEED TECHNICAL DOCUMENTATION – WHERE DO YOU GO FOR COURTEOUS SERVICE AND PROFESSIONALISM?

- Software technical authorship
- Laser printing
- Business systems consultancy
- Publications management
- Author training

marlow durndell

Bahnhofstrasse,
Zurich
CH8001 Switzerland.

Advertisement

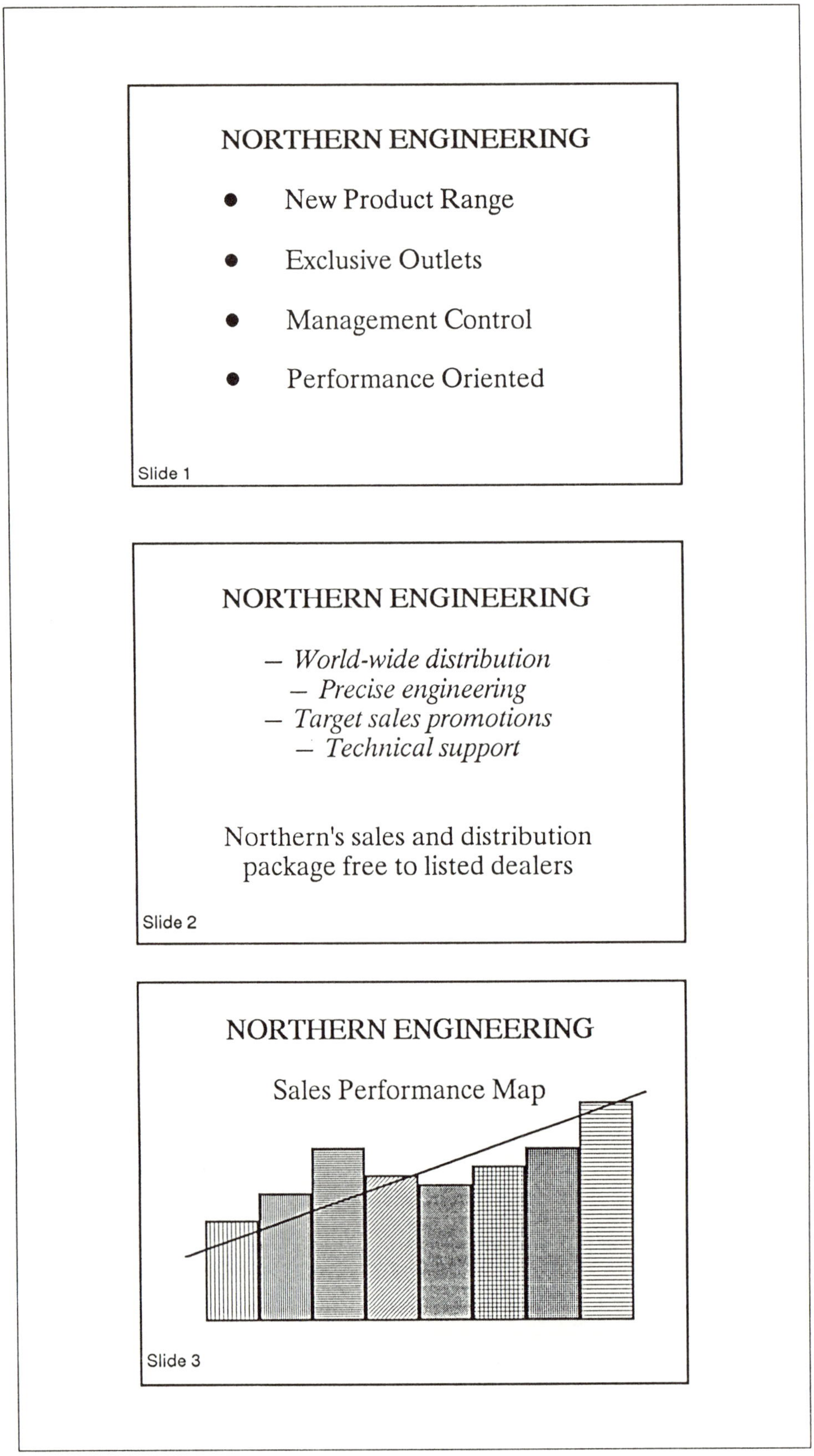

Audio Visual Slides/Transparencies

This is to Certify that
MARY BONNINGTON

has successfully completed a

Business Communication

course, with distinction

Dated this first day of June, 1990

Course supervisor ____________

Administrator ____________

Certificate

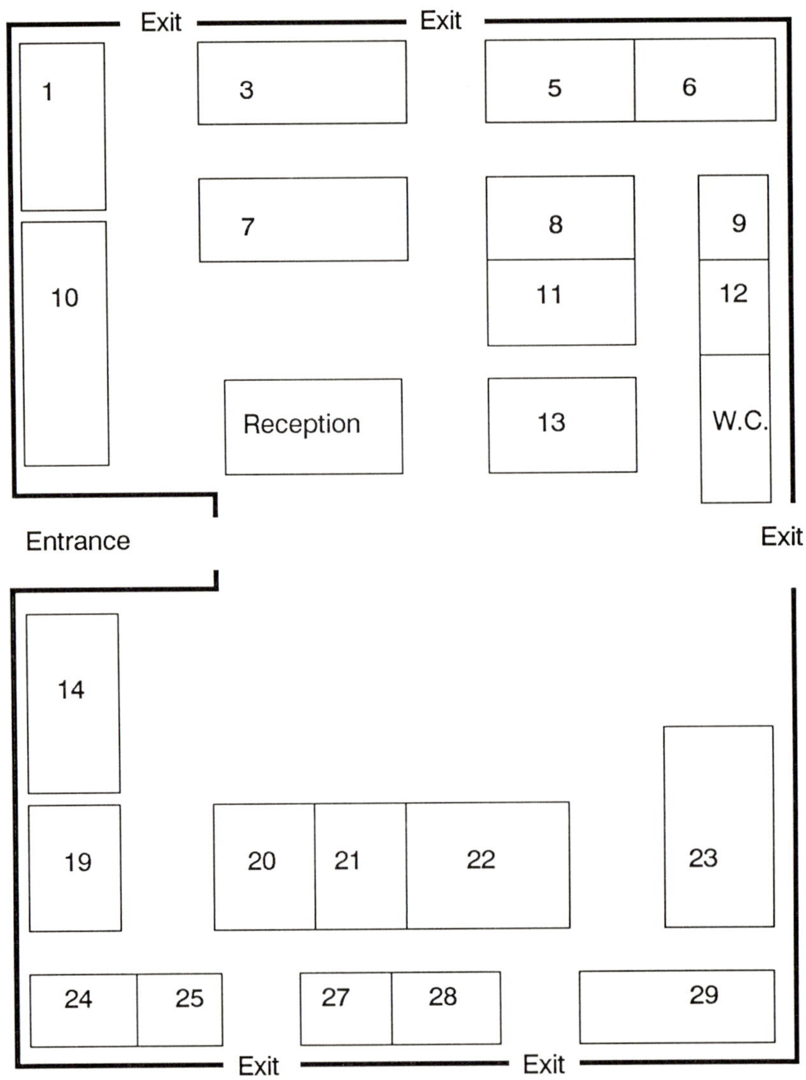

List of Exhibitors

1 Murrey International
3 Hawksley Finance
5 Winter Brewer Limited
6 Harvey Cowell Industries
7 Bellmond Group
8 Applethorpe Limited
9 C T Billingham
10 New England Traders Corp.
11 Pullman Group
12 Uxbridge Newsprint Limited
13 Muller Fischer GmbH
14 Vercross Bros.
19 Schula & Sons
20 Mable Carter
21 Dewhurst Limited
22 Parkbridge Group
23 Medina Finance
24 Parabola Print
25 W S Drage
27 Newhope Design
28 Trent Banking
29 Walther Konig

Plan

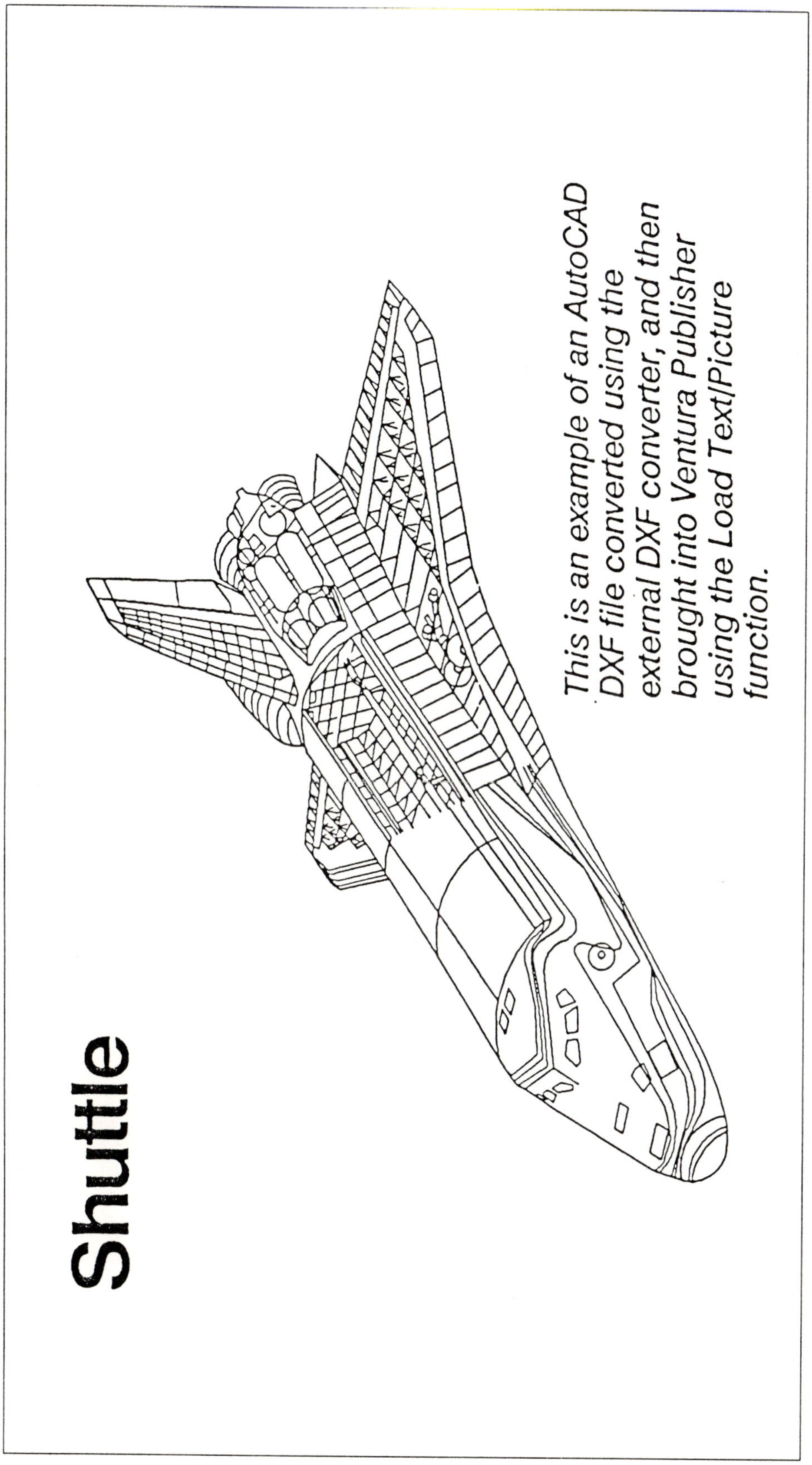

Design Drawings

Company Name

Sales Report for 3rd Quarter

Lorem ipsum dolor sit amet, consectetuer adipiscing elit, sed diam nonummy nibh euismod tincidunt ut laoreet dolore magna aliquam erat volutpat. Ut wisi enim ad minim veniam, quis nostrud exerci tation ullamcorper suscipit lobortis nisl ut aliquip ex ea commodo consequat.

Vel eum iriure dolor in hendrerit in vulputate velit esse molestie consequat, vel illum dolore eu feugiat nulla facilisis at vero eros et accumsan et iusto odio dignissim qui blandit praesent luptatum zzril delenit augue duis dolore te feugait nulla facilisi.

Lorem ipsum dolor sit amet, consectetuer adipiscing elit, sed diam nonummy nibh euismod tincidunt ut laoreet dolore magna aliquam erat volutpat. Ut wisi enim ad minim veniam, quis nostrud exerci tation ullamcorper suscipit lobortis nisl ut aliquip ex ea commodo consequat. Duis autem vel eum iriure dolor in hendrerit in vulputate velit esse molestie consequat, vel illum dolore eu feugiat nulla facilisis at vero eros et accumsan et iusto odio dignissim qui blandit praesent luptatum zzril delenit augue duis dolore te feugait nulla facilisi.

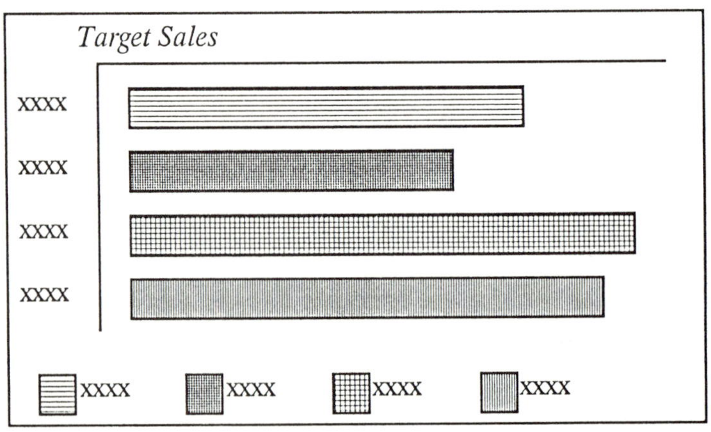

Lorem ipsum dolor sit amet, consectetuer adipiscing elit, sed diam nonummy nibh euismod tincidunt ut laoreet dolore magna aliquam erat volutpat. Ut wisi enim ad minim veniam, quis nostrud exerci tation ullamcorper suscipit lobortis nisl ut aliquip ex ea commodo consequat.

Duis autem vel eum iriure dolor in hendrerit in vulputate velit esse molestie consequat, vel illum dolore eu feugiat

Sales Report

2

Business Reply Service 90812314

Panda Products Limited
P O Box 2143
Newtown
Hampshire
H10 5ST

Name ....

Telephone ....

Address..
....
....
....
....
....

Please fold along dotted lines

I would like more information on: ....

....

....

....

Reply-paid Card

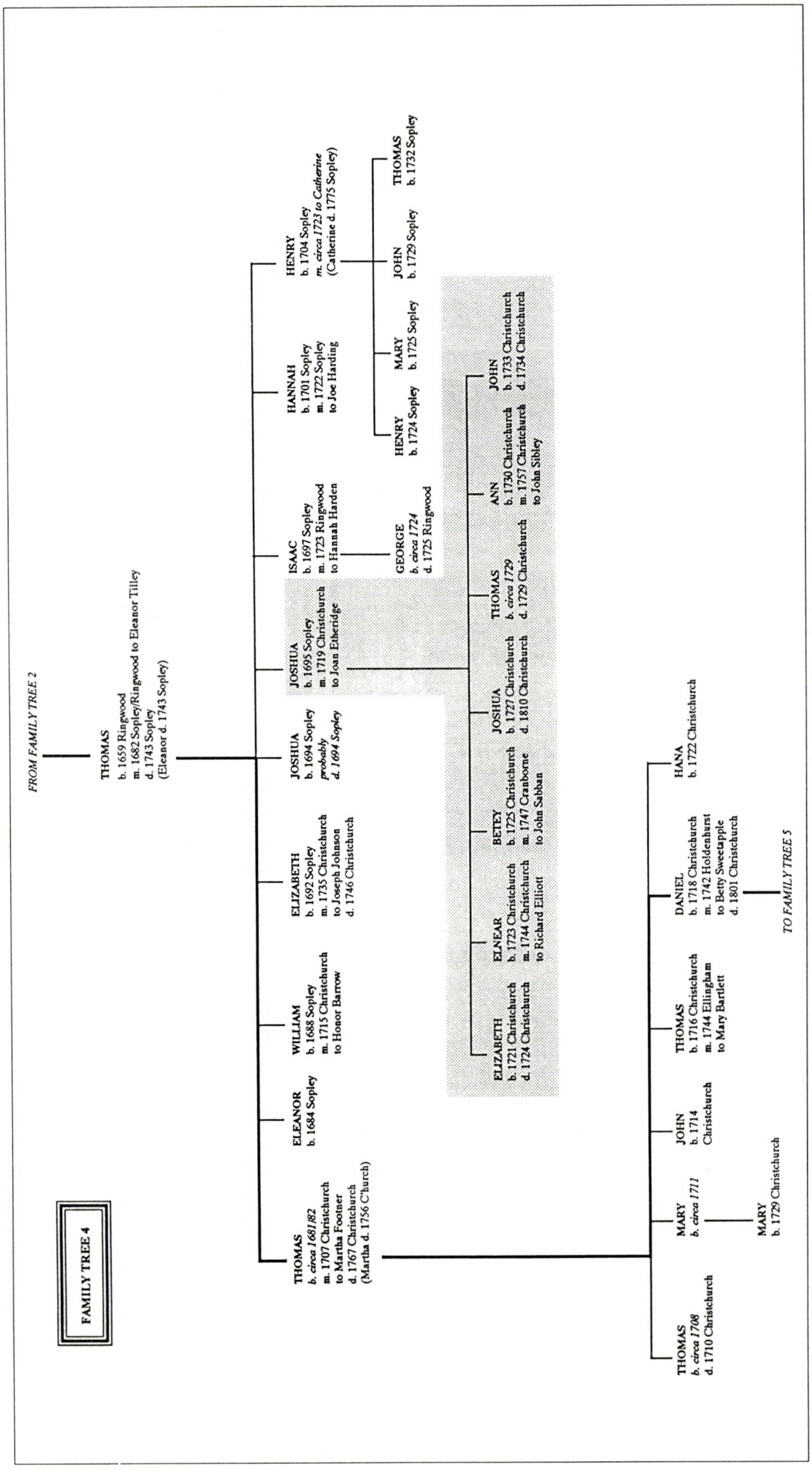

FAMILY TREE 4
FROM FAMILY TREE 2
THOMAS b. 1659 Ringwood m. 1682 Sopley/Ringwood to Eleanor Tilley d. 1743 Sopley (Eleanor d. 1743 Sopley)
THOMAS b. circa 1681/82 m. 1707 Christchurch to Martha Footner d. 1767 Christchurch (Martha d. 1756 C'hurch)
ELEANOR b. 1684 Sopley
WILLIAM b. 1688 Sopley m. 1715 Christchurch to Honor Barrow
ELIZABETH b. 1692 Sopley m. 1735 Christchurch to Joseph Johnson d. 1746 Christchurch
JOSHUA b. 1694 Sopley probably d. 1694 Sopley
JOSHUA b. 1695 Sopley m. 1719 Christchurch to Joan Etheridge
ISAAC b. 1697 Sopley m. 1723 Ringwood to Hannah Harden
HANNAH b. 1701 Sopley m. 1722 Sopley to Joe Harding
HENRY b. 1704 Sopley m. circa 1723 to Catherine (Catherine d. 1775 Sopley)
GEORGE b. circa 1724 d. 1725 Ringwood
HENRY b. 1724 Sopley
MARY b. 1725 Sopley
JOHN b. 1729 Sopley
THOMAS b. 1732 Sopley
ELIZABETH b. 1721 Christchurch d. 1724 Christchurch
ELNEAR b. 1723 Christchurch m. 1744 Christchurch to Richard Elliott
BETEY b. 1725 Christchurch m. 1747 Cranborne to John Sabban
JOSHUA b. 1727 Christchurch d. 1810 Christchurch
THOMAS b. circa 1729 d. 1729 Christchurch
ANN b. 1730 Christchurch m. 1757 Christchurch to John Sibley
JOHN b. 1733 Christchurch d. 1734 Christchurch
THOMAS b. circa 1708 d. 1710 Christchurch
MARY b. circa 1711
MARY b. 1729 Christchurch
JOHN b. 1714 Christchurch
THOMAS b. 1716 Christchurch m. 1744 Ellingham to Mary Bartlett
DANIEL b. 1718 Christchurch m. 1742 Holdenhurst to Betty Sweetapple d. 1801 Christchurch
HANA b. 1722 Christchurch
TO FAMILY TREE 5

Family Tree

Menu

• • • • • • • •

Soups

Consommé de volaille

Consommé printanier

Soupe aux truffes Élysée

Soupe ardennaise

Fish

Filets de barbue grillés Saint-Germain

Daurade

Fricandeau d'esturgeon

Haddock ou aiglefin fumé

Brandade de morue à la ménagère

Meat

Châteaubriant

Coeur de filet sauté ou grille

Boeuf à la mode

Cuisse de boeuf rôtie au feu de bois

Restaurant Menu

Index